From Brokenness to Wholeness

The
Daffney Michè Hawkins' Story

DAFFNEY M. HAWKINS

From Brokenness to Wholeness

The
Daffney Michè Hawkins' Story

Single, Married, Separated and Divorced
Never Give Up!

DAFFNEY M. HAWKINS

NUVISION PUBLISHING
2019

Scriptures are taken from The Holy Bible
(Public Domain)

Books may be ordered through booksellers
or by contacting:
www.thekingministry.org

First Printing: 2019

ISBN 978-0-578-21966-0

NuVision Publishing
PO Box 4455 | Wilmington, NC 28406
www.nuvisiondesigns.biz/publications

Printed in the United States of America.

DEDICATIONS

This book is dedicated to:

- The Lord Christ Jesus, for His unfailing love and support. I am enamored by Your Holy Presence in my life.

- My three sons Toney DeWayne Sampson, Travis DeWhite Sampson and Teron DeWitt Sampson. I am proud to call you my sons. I love you guys very much. Each of you are my greatest accomplishments in life. I am so blessed to be your mother.

- My Brenda – My beautiful daughter-in-love – Publicly, welcome to our family. You are so easy to love. Our praise and worship times are out of this world. Oh, I do not want to be remised – Our girls' getaway weekends are loaded with truckloads of fun and plenty of good food. Thank you for being you!

- To my brothers, I have always loved you.

In Loving Memory of my Parents

- The late Elder Nehemiah Dean and the late Mother Dorothy Olinda Smith. I love you guys. Honor is due to you both. Thank you for being my parents!

TABLE OF CONTENTS

ACKNOWLEDGMENTS 9

FOREWORD 11

INTRODUCTION 13

Chapter One: PAIN: THE EXPRESSION OF BROKENNESS 15

Chapter Two: MAKE A NEW SOUND...29

Chapter Three: WHO ARE YOU? 41

Chapter Four: GOD KNOWS WHO YOU ARE! 53

Chapter Five: REST FOR MY SOUL 65

Chapter Six: REACHING HIGHER HEIGHTS............................79

Chapter Seven: WHERE IS THAT SOUND COMING FROM?.......91

Chapter Eight: VICTORIOUS LIVING IN CHRIST JESUS 103

Chapter Nine: NOW, IT'S TIME TO SOAR! 115

Chapter Ten: LIVING YOUR BEST LIFE AND ENJOYING
YOURSELF 127

Chapter Eleven: FORGETTING YOUR PAST AND MOVING
FORWARD 137

Chapter Twelve: THANK YOU MOMMIE 149

FROM BROKENNESS TO WHOLENESS................................... 159

SCRIPTURE REFERENCE.. 161

ACKNOWLEDGMENTS

- Thank you, Bishop Ross and First Lady Brenda Jackson, Sr. for believing in the God who is living within me. Thanks for your love, support and encouragement.

- Thanks to Ana, Karen and Theresa - Thank you ladies for your willingness to serve as my editors. I appreciate your dedication, devotion and diligence. I am blessed by your kindness and support.

- A special thanks to Karen - You are a work of class. You are an Editor at heart! Thanks for reading and editing large amounts of data. Whenever I called, emailed or texted, you promptly answered. Words can't express how much I appreciate your assistance and encouragement.

- Thanks to Carolyn and Christine who served as the focus group participants and final editors. Thank you both for generously giving your time, attention and feedback.

- To my publisher, Lola (NuVision Publishing) – Thank you from the bottom of my heart. You went above and beyond the call of duty. Thanks for your prayers and encouragement.

- To everyone who prayed for me and read portions of my book manuscript – God bless you and know that you are not forgotten.

- To the Only the King Can Do It Ministry, Inc. staff – I love you ladies. You guys are the best. Thanks for your love, prayers, support, and assistance. I enjoy spreading the good news of Christ Jesus with you.

- To my dearest Sisters-In-Christ who are my friends - It is wonderful to have a relationship with such a diverse group of ladies. Thank you for your warm hugs, acknowledgements and the deepest expression of love. During some of my weakest moments, you guys poured out prayers for me. Your encouragement, inspirations and gifts continue to lift me up. You guys believed in me. I am blessed to have you all in my life.

- To my family members who prayed and supported me, I have nothing but love for you.

- Jackie – Thanks for showing me hospitality when I needed a safe and quiet place to write a significant portion of my book. I knew by the smile on your face that it was your pleasure.

- Kathleen - Many years ago, you spoke prophetic words to me about my future. You stated that my story would one day help others, and that God had a plan for my life. Thank you for being so kind to me.

- Doreé - Although you are my friend, thank you for being the mother that I longed for, and the sister I never had. I am grateful for our friendship!

FOREWORD

written by Bishop Ross Jackson, Sr.

The book you are about to read is not only true but, incredibly relevant. Daffney Hawkins' story is one that will help us realize that we all are broken in one way or another. Humanity has been broken from its origin. Our wholeness comes from being one with our Maker. It's in Him that we live, move and have our being. Daffney's story is one of pain and suffering, but it is also one of overcoming and triumph. Without the leading and guidance of the Holy Spirit, we find ourselves lost. We often find ourselves wandering through life as ships without a sail. While wandering without guidance, we fall into traps and snares set by Satan.

The enemy of our souls is the author of confusion that tries to destroy us by any means necessary. Satan knows if he can infiltrate our minds and plant seeds of doubt and despair; we will be trapped in a mental prison without the hope that God intended for us. We cannot fall into this trap. We must follow the instructions found in God's Word. We have a helper in the Holy Spirit who was sent for the purpose of leading and guiding us to all truth. The truth is we are more than conquerors through Christ who strengthens us. The truth is we were born to have hope, not despair.

Daffney's story is our story as well. Like her, we can all come to our senses and return to God, our Father, and find peace. I am so grateful to God for giving Daffney the courage to write this book for our sake. Her transparency and candor will help to set many free.

Love you daughter,
Bishop Dr. Ross M. Jackson, Sr.
Overseer of Christian Hearts Fellowship Ministries

INTRODUCTION

For many years, there was an excruciating pain within my heart. My life was not supposed to be like this. I thought, "Is this a nightmare?" Then, why can't I wake-up? Please someone wake me up. During my childhood and a portion of my adult life, I was broken. Each waking moment meant the search was on to discover "wholeness." A place where I could rest and not be overly concerned about anything. Why can't I find this place? Why does it feel like my whole world is shaken apart? These are some of the overwhelming questions that bombarded my mind.

My name is Daffney Miché Hawkins, and I am a born-again believer of Christ Jesus. I am so in love with God. I can't stop thanking Him for all He has done for me. He has rescued me from many emotional and adverse situations. For countless years, I disliked myself and the broken status that I carried in life. Appalling thoughts raked my mind such as "If only I would have done this or that...or Why was I so stupid?" I was clothed with blame, condemnation, and many other destructive emotions. Psychologically, my mind was a mess.

I felt obligated for some strange reason to carry the faults and burdens of other people. I know what you are thinking - Bondage 101. There was a mystifying problem that dwelled deep inside of me.

My escape from Brokenness to Wholeness came in the form of total surrender and forgiveness. The harvest from them provided the fortitude to genuinely forgive those who afflicted tremendous pain on me. It just so happened that one of my offenders was my own Mother. Now I must confess, it took a little longer to forgive my mama. Wasn't she the one who was supposed to love and protect me? Mama contributed to a great amount of my struggles.

As I progressed towards wholeness, I conditioned my ears to listen and analyze my inner thoughts. I was conscious and cognizant to every thought which entered my mind. The Holy Spirit helped me to distinguish healthy and unhealthy ones. It is amazing how God's light can shine in the deepest and darkest places of our existence. God healed and left me with a beautiful scar – my testimony. It is my personal reminder of how good He is. God always builds up, and He never tears down. The enemy always tears down, and he never builds up.

Shortly, you will read about my personal testimony. I share some of my saddest trials and triumphant breakthroughs. You will discover that each chapter is woven with portions of them. My poignant stories are filled with meaningful information, sound advice and effective techniques. In order to receive the full understanding of them, I ask you to read the entire book. When God does something good, it's hard to keep it to yourself. I pray that this book will be used as an instrument for hope and restoration.

Get a cup of water, tea or coffee because…From Brokenness to Wholeness starts now!

CHAPTER ONE
PAIN: THE EXPRESSION
OF BROKENNESS

God sets the solitary in families;
He brings out those who are bound into prosperity;
(Psalm 68:6)

On February 22nd in the District of Columbia at D.C. General Hospital, I came into the earth's atmosphere and took my first breath. Before my grandiose appearance, my parents Nehemiah Dean Jr. and Dorothy Olinda Smith had two previous sons: Duncan Aaron (Dunk) and Deane Fitzgerald (Gerald). When my parents became pregnant with their third child, they strongly wished for a daughter. They felt that a little girl could help soften things up within their family. Heaven honored their petition by blessing them with a healthy and beautiful baby girl. My presence exhilarated their hearts with pure joy.

Prior to my birth, one of my maternal cousins was in an interracial relationship. His girlfriend's name was Daphne. Mama fell in love with that name and vowed to give it to her first-born female child. True to her word, I was named Daffney Miché Smith. Mama spelled my first name in a unique way. My parents noticed how my eyes sparkled like bright stars, so I was given the nickname of Twinkles. One of my maternal great aunts jokingly laughed at them, for they did not attend special outings for almost a year. They were a bit overjoyed by the arrival of their baby girl! Three years later, Daddy and Mama welcomed my younger brother, Darrin Anthony (Tony). My parents were satisfied and decided to close-up the shop. They felt everyone who was supposed to be born had arrived.

Things were said to be almost normal as I went through infancy to toddlerhood. Not everyone in my household rejoicefully embraced my presence. Prior to my birth, my middle brother, Gerald, carried the title as "the baby of the family." This meant that some of the spot light was removed from him and placed directly on me. Well, he was not a happy camper. He felt that he was being dethroned from his position by the likes of me.

My mother stated how she sat me in a baby carrier seat and stationed me on top of our dining room table. Momentarily, she stepped out of the room to grab something. As she returned back into the room my dear brother, Gerald was on one of the dining room chairs with the intention to pull me off the table onto the floor. The little rascal got caught, and my mother prevented my fall. Thanks Mom!

At age four, I was enrolled into a pre-Kindergarten daycare center. A lot of the school-aged neighborhood children attended the before and after care program. The teachers watched us like a hawk. I will never forget an incident that I encountered with one of them. It is amazing how I can vividly remember it. It took place in the cafeteria during breakfast time. A tray of food was placed before me. Little did I know that a foreign substance would be included on it. I heard someone refer to it as "oatmeal." "Huh," I thought, "what's that?" It had a repulsive look, and I didn't like how its substance stuck together. I continued to gape at the oatmeal.

After a while, I became curious about the oatmeal. There were ambiguous thoughts of unattractiveness that plummeted my mind, but I decided to taste it. I put a nominal portion of it into my mouth. Let's just say I was not pleased. The texture of the oatmeal was soft and slimy. I thought it was one of the most horrible foods I had ever tasted on the planet Earth. I knew that I could not eat any more of it.

I slid the bowl of oatmeal to the side, ate my fruit and drank my milk. I got up to discard my leftover food and empty containers into the trash can. The daycare teacher said to me in a very harsh tone, "you cannot throw that food away. You must eat the oatmeal before you go outside to play." I lowered my head and walked defeatedly back to my table.

I felt hurt and dejected as the other children ate and finished their oatmeal. Joyfully, they went outside to play. I sat for a good while which meant time was subtracted from my playtime. For a four-year-old, this was an unpleasant position to be placed in. That mean and irritable teacher repeated her words, "you can't go outside until you finish eating your oatmeal." It was like she received pleasure by forcing me to do something against my will.

She continued to stare at me. I knew I wasn't going to eat the yucky oatmeal, so my young mind started to devise a strategy. I concocted a brilliant plan – I would place it into my empty milk carton. Then, it happened. My daycare teacher got distracted. Quickly, I shoveled the oatmeal into my milk carton. It worked. After I passed her inspection, she allowed me to get up from the table, discard all of my empty containers and go outdoors to play on the daycare playground area.

The same day, I arrived home and shared the above-mentioned occurrence with my parents. My mama was not happy that one of the teachers attempted to forcefully make me eat the oatmeal. (emphatically not pleased at all). She let it be known by a discontented expression on her face. I was removed from that daycare center because of that foreign substance called "oatmeal" and my teacher's harsh words. I bet my mother had some interesting things to say to those folks at the daycare center. As an adult, I still do not like oatmeal. Whenever I see it, I smile and recall that awful childhood memory.

After my graduation from kindergarten, my parents decided that they wanted to move their family to a safer and better environment. We moved from a two-bedroom apartment unit in Washington, D.C. (Stanton Road, SE) to a semi-detached townhouse in the suburb of Prince George's County, Maryland. For the first time, my parents were homeowners. The move offered us additional living space and a higher quality of education. My parents were delighted to have a fenced front and back yard that their children could play in. This was the reason why we were able to get two pet dogs. Our first dog was named Puncho. He was a mixed breed (Border Terrier and miniature Poodle) with fluffy white hair.

After our beloved Puncho passed away, my family welcomed the beautiful Faygo. She was a fluffy black-and-tan mixed dog (Border Terrier, miniature Poodle and Cocker Spaniel) with an attitude of "I know that I am gorgeous." Faygo looked exactly like the dog in the Benji movies (for the younger readers, google it). Both of our dogs were indoor pets and greatly loved. I am laughing because many people who visited us were amused at how our house didn't have an animal odor. Mama made sure we kept those dogs spick and span.

Many years later, Dunk told me that our new area felt like living in the country. The places were spaced apart and required an automobile. He preferred the city life because it offered more activities and convenient transit methods to access them.

Our three-bedroom townhouse was located on Sherriff Road, Landover, Maryland. A busy intersection in a middle-class neighborhood located in the community of Palmer Park. One side of the street was townhouses and situated on the opposite side was a 300-acre farm. The farm was called "Wilson Farm." It was owned by generations of Wilson family members. It was richly maintained and occupied by farm workers and different kinds of animals, especially cows. There were lots of them! I remember there were days when the stench of the cows' manure permeated our entire neighborhood area. I mean from miles away people smelled this horrible odor. On those days, we did not leave our front screen door open.

The farm property was restricted and had "no trespassing" signs displayed around their land. We were told how some people who disobeyed and violated the warning signs were prosecuted and received huge fines. I didn't directly know of anyone who received such a fine. Due to the strict policy of the farm, many of the neighborhood children were afraid to cross the street. The fear didn't stop some children from retrieving balls or other objects that were thrown inadvertently. I was a bit curious about it, but I never ventured off to walk on the grounds of that farm. Many years later, the Wilson farm was sold. You might know one of its occupants; it is the home to the Washington Redskins football team's FedEx Field.

I attended William Paca Elementary School. It was located a couple of short blocks from where I lived on the same side as the Wilson's farm. It was a one-level red-bricked building with narrow hallways. I was an average student who was shy. I didn't have a lot of girlfriends. At times, I observed a certain popular group of girls' interactions. I was not given an invitation to join them. They only gravitated to each other. One of them was the leader of the group. She was given respect and influence over the rest of the girls. Moreover, she dictated and commanded what the group would do and say. In my mind, I can still see that popular group of girls walking and playing on the school playground. If the leader stopped walking, they stopped too. If the leader ran, they ran too. If the leader didn't talk to certain people, they did not talk to those people either. Well, by now, you get it. The leader of this group had her followers well-trained.

On occasions in the lunchroom, I sat at their table. No one really noticed me. The popular group of girls enjoyed talking, laughing and sharing certain childhood topics. Their chatter filled the cafeteria. I did not join in their group discussions, for I was invisible to them. I wanted to be a part of their camaraderie. However, it did not make sense to my young mind why the girls needed to follow and be bossed around by a leader. This was one of the main reasons why I did not want to join their group. As an alternative, I decided to hang with a skeleton group of girls. There was no leader in our group.

The most highlighted and eventful time was my sixth grade graduation. The teachers and my sixth grade classmates were filled with glee. The program was properly planned and advertised. My parents expressed words of congratulations to me. My mom purchased a cute wide leg light blue and white jumpsuit for me to wear; it had the cutest little cape. Mama was very proud of that outfit. The morning of my special event, I was filled with excitement as I put on my new outfit. God knows I felt like a beautiful princess. It was a wonderful graduation ceremony that was filled with lots of applauds and smiles from the students, parents and school faculty personnel.

My middle school was called Kent Junior High School located in Palmer Park, Maryland. Since I lived within the proximity of the school, I was classified as a walker. There were some children who were bused from different cities throughout the Prince George's County areas. The parking lot of the school was very busy with lots of buses, and the students were noisy and excited as they walked into the building and were greeted by their friends. The children came from different ethnic groups and socio-economic classes. I loved it. It opened the door to meet new people who didn't look like me and had dissimilar backgrounds.

Junior High provided me with a bit of freedom. There were mornings that some of the neighborhood children and I walked to school. It took us less than a half hour to reach the school building. As we passed by the creek, recreation center, and a shopping center, we talked and laughed about various teenage subjects of interest. Other times, I walked to school alone. I valued my alone time, for it gave me a chance to think about the perplexities of life. I wondered, "Why did God created us? and What was the true meaning of our existence on Earth?" I surmised that life was like a play. Each person had a special role to play. When I walked alone, there was no need to hurry to keep up with the other children. I had more time to stop by one of the shopping center stores to purchase my favorite snack (barbecue flavored potato chips). I still remember the rich favor.

I was pleasantly surprised that junior high classes were structured differently than my elementary ones. There were a lot of them. I was given a class schedule that listed teachers' names and classroom numbers. Moreover, I was assigned to report to a homeroom classroom for attendance only. Each classroom meant different teachers and classmates. It took a while to learn my way around the building. I came to the startling conclusion that I graduated from elementary school to gain more responsibilities in middle school.

My grades were average. My parents gave little encouragement and interest regarding my academic achievements. I was not asked questions like "what occurred at school or which assignments were due?" There was one expectation they enforced pertaining to school; I had to pass all classes. I am not condoning their actions, as their minds were on paying the household bills and other things.

Their children's education was not a top priority, for it was pushed behind their bills. Life is something.

I loved my English classes. I did exceptionally well in them. I remember one of my assignments was to write an essay about my summer vacation. I selected to write about our family trip to New York. I was determined to write about a story filled with excitement and adventure. The dialogue for my story was easy to generate, as some of my maternal family members lived in Long Island, New York. Whenever we visited them, there was never a dull moment.

One of my middle school English teachers, Ms. Ableton, was very impressed with my writing project. I received an excellent grade. She asked my mother to encourage me to go to the University of Maryland to major in English. Little did Ms. Ableton know, that my mother was not interested in my education. She never even asked me what I wanted to be when I grew up. Furthermore, my mother thought higher learning made people pompous.

I became extremely fearful of my English classes. New concepts were introduced, and I had a tough time as I attempted to grasp them. Then out of nowhere, negative thoughts of inadequacy mounted up within my mind. I listened, believed and followed them. My attention was diverted from excelling in English classes and replaced with thoughts of incompetency. I felt like a failure. I did not share my thoughts of ignorance with my parents or English teachers. Therefore, they were neatly tucked away in one of my compartments within my subliminal mind.

I attended Parkdale High School in Lanham, Maryland. The neighborhood was considered upper middle-class. My goodness, those folks had some beautiful houses! At school, I enjoyed my classes and hung out with a group of close friends. We had great chemistry. We waited and greeted each other before our morning classes. We ate lunch together and had various conversations throughout the day. We would even hang by each other's lockers and place certain items into them. At times, we found isolated stairways to talk and laugh about the silliest of things. They were cool to hang with. It was the first time that I truly felt welcomed and had a sense of belonging.

Sometimes, we hung around each other outside of school. We thought that we were going to be together forever. One day a guidance counselor had a friendly conversation with us. He told us when we become adults there might be a possibility that we could separate. My friends and I adamantly denied his words and counted them as lies. The audacity of him to say such things. We were going to remain friends forever. As of today, I have no idea where they are. The guidance counselor was right. There is a song from the movie "Grease" entitled "We Go Together." Every time I hear it, I laugh and think about my high school friends.

After my junior year in high school, we moved to Gateway Blvd. in District Heights, Maryland. I loved our new home. It was beautifully designed and decorated. Our neighborhood was quieter and prettier. Each house in our neighborhood had its own unique characteristics. Most of them had patios; they were different sizes and had long driveways. The children were hardly seen playing in their front yards, that may explain why the front lawns were so immaculate.

One thing that I didn't like was how the neighbors did not appear as friendly as the folks on Sheriff Road. When I started at my new school, Suitland High School, it was very organized. They offered more after school activities than Parkdale High School did. Also, they had an open lunch program. For one hour, students had permission to depart off the grounds of the school. This was also offered at my previous school. However, after I got transferred to my new school, my former High School abolished their open lunch policy. I felt very lucky to be at Suitland!

Many of my classmates were polite to their teachers and focused on their classwork. They stayed within their own pocket of friendships. This made it difficult to meet new people. It was unfortunate for me because my friends were at Parkdale High School. Nevertheless, I was very thankful to God to meet a girl named Maria. We became good friends and even to the present day, we are still friends.

I didn't attend my high school prom. Therefore, I didn't get to experience dress shopping with my mother. Honestly, I didn't really care. My relationship with an ex-boyfriend had ended abruptly and painfully. He broke my heart. Days after the break-up, I went to the guidance office to ask some questions pertaining to my classes. I noticed a sign hanging on one of the walls. It said, "if you love something, let it go. If it was meant to be, it will come back. If it doesn't, it never was." These words went straight to my heart in a prolific way. Because of them, I was able to release my first love.

The day after my prom, a lot of the students shared what a great time they had. They talked about partying hard, excessive drinking and getting their groove on. As I listened to them, I knew that I didn't miss anything of value.

There was something that I truly wanted, a class ring. I was given a catalog which displayed different styles of rings. When I saw the ones offered to females, I was elated. Former graduate seniors wore their class rings with dignity. Now, it was my turn. Have you ever heard the old phrase that says what goes up must come down? When I looked at the prices of those rings, I was flabbergasted, for the rings were more than a hundred dollars. More than a hundred dollars....that was a lot of money. It didn't make sense to my teenage mind. How in the world could a ring be over one hundred dollars? It would have taken me three to four paychecks to purchase it. This truly bothered me. I didn't have the nerve to ask Mama and Daddy for the money. Therefore, I didn't buy a class ring.

After my high school graduation, one of my girlfriends and I went to eat at Red Lobster. She wanted to celebrate my accomplishment. Sadly, this was the extent of my graduation celebration. There was no family celebratory dinner or any gifts. I can recall how excited my mother was that I graduated without getting pregnant. My mama felt this was a huge accomplishment. Years later, it was revealed why she was ecstatic (to be discussed in a later chapter).

After high school, I didn't go to college. I figured that I had been in school for twelve years and "enough was enough." Mama and Daddy were satisfied with my high school diploma. My mother dropped out of school when she was in the ninth grade, and my papa left school when he was a junior in high school. I never knew the benefits of pursuing a higher education until, I became an adult.

Finally, I was able to make my own decisions. It was time for me to tread into unfamiliar territory, so off I went to work in the corporate world. In retrospect, I was naïve and unprepared for it.

Digging deeper into the Core of my Pain

During my childhood, my mother was the center of our family. She made sure her children were fed, cleaned and dressed neatly. However, she did not provide the emotional stability we needed. Our home was her oasis; and she cleaned it a lot. Then, she would talk about what a fantastic job she did. I hated when she cleaned the house. Mama complained as she vacuumed every room that had carpet. In different rooms, she swept and left piles of trash in the middle of the floors. Then, her attention was diverted to something else. She spent a lot of time and effort as she dusted almost every item in the entire house. I remembered how my father would step over piles of trash as he walked through our house. He quickly got out of her way.

Moreover, my mother would move things out of place and clean every nook and cranny. The rooms looked like tornados after she moved everything out of its place to thoroughly clean. It took hours on top of hours for her to complete all the cleaning tasks. Everything had to be perfect. In hindsight, she made more work for herself and blamed it on everyone else in the house for not offering to help. Her negative energy filled the whole house. The atmosphere was disturbed and filled with dread. This made it a very unhappy place to live.

When she cleaned my room, she made me feel like a filthy and trifling human being. I was not a sloppy child nor a clean freak. Mama would spend a very long time cleaning my bedroom. She found strength to move my sturdy bed and find the smallest pieces of papers on my floor. This made her angry at me. Next, she had to go through all of my bedroom dresser drawers. If there were any dust particles, she found them.

Everything inside the drawers had to be removed, folded, and neatly tucked away. My mother's mouth was filthy, and she cussed almost as bad as a sailor. As she cleaned, her face had a distorted frown on it. As she used profanity and complained against me, (please excuse my French) I was called a "bitch" and a "heifer." Who does that? No mother should ever call her daughter these degrading names.

I wished that she would hurry up and get out of my room. But she had to clean my closet too. All my clothing had to be neatly placed on hangers, and my shoes had to be properly in place. It was sickening. My mother's words were like daggers. They pierced right through my tender, young heart. I rehearsed within my mind how I was supposed to hate her for the harsh treatment she gave to me. Then guilt filled my mind, and I felt disturbed in my young mind - I didn't like the negative way I thought about my mama. I knew that God would be displeased with me. Sadly, I had nobody to discuss her inappropriate and disrespectful behavior with.

This was the initial start of my introduction to the painful effect of negative and critical words. I heard an adage that went like this "sticks and stones may break my bones, but words will never hurt me." As a child I kept saying them verbally, but they didn't take a profound effect within me. I carried my mother's harmful verbal attacks for many years.

Although my father did not approve of her using these words, my mama continued to speak in an inappropriate manner. As a young female child, I craved for her friendship and to hear her say the words "I love you." I wanted to hear my mother give positive words of affirmation. I wanted her to say how proud she was of me. I longed to be wrapped in her arms. I wanted to feel safe.

A Journey back to my Childhood

In my mind, I am taking a concise trip back into my past. You are invited to join me as I share what I see. I am reliving my bedroom dilemma. I can vividly see that hurt little girl. I am afraid, shaken and baffled. I wish I could hug her and let my younger self know that everything will be alright. The look on my face is filled with terror. I am watching my mother as she franticly snatches my clothes and personal items out of my dresser drawers onto the floor. Mama looks like a wild woman. She is making a huge mess and complaining about how messy and trifling I am. My mother stops to look at me with eyes of disdain. It is as if she doesn't love me. God knows the look in her eyes causes me to want to run and hide behind a rock.

No, I will not run away from the terror of my mother's hatred. I have decided to speak up for that broken little girl. As an adult, I can articulate my thoughts.

Dear Mommie,

Why are you so mean to me? I am the same baby girl who you brought into this world. You welcomed me with open arms. You loved me at first sight. You clothed and fed me. You gently held and rocked me in your arms. You were very proud and filled with gratitude that God gave you a little baby doll. What happened, Mama? Why do I feel nothing but pain and hurt from the very person who birthed me into the world? Mom, why did you change your behavior towards me? In some capacity, did I dampen your dreams? Did I become a hardship to our family? Why don't I make you happy anymore? I am so sorry that I disappointed you. – Please tell me how to eliminate the things that you don't like about me. I promise to work diligently to remove them. Mama, I want you to be proud to be my mother. But for now, Mama please - I beg and plead for your love, approval and acceptance. Don't mistreat me – Because, I need you.

With love,
Your one and only Daughter
Twinkles

CHAPTER TWO
MAKE A NEW SOUND

Enter into His gates with thanksgiving, and into His courts with
praise. Be thankful to Him, and bless His name
(Psalm 100:4)

Portrait of Intimacy

David was a well-known Jewish King from the tribe of Judah
(symbolizes praise). Who happened to be a musician, poet and
warrior. He was the second king of Israel. The Holy Bible states
that he was a rich man and an extraordinary king. He had many
wives; eight of them are named. With his wives (except for one), he
had 19 sons and one daughter. David had countless other children
with his concubines. That brother was a busy man.

The king prayed, praised and worshiped constantly to the Lord.
Yet, he was not a perfect man. David committed some egregious
sins, whether they were intentional or unintentional, he confessed
his transgressions and sought-after God's forgiveness. God
graciously extended His grace and mercy toward his son. King
David's heart pointed and pounded for the true and living God. The
Heavenly Father gave him the title of "a man after My Own Heart."
God loved David, and David loved Him. Their devotion and
commitment to each other was based on trust.

When David was a young shepherd boy, he meticulously guarded his father, Jesse's sheep. He didn't view it as a tedious and meaningless position. He took pride at how he performed his shepherd responsibilities. Each sheep was given love, care, and affection. He protected them from ravenous and atrocious animals. He mentions how he killed a lion and a bear with his bare hands. The shepherd boy spent a large quantity of quality time alone, conversing with the lover of His soul. The Father imparted wisdom, knowledge, and understanding to him. He downloaded profound details about His character into David's heart. Through the brightest of days or the starriest of nights, he was not lonely. David knew that God was with him.

David was an anointed musician. There is an interesting biblical story about him and his predecessor King Saul from the tribe of Benjamin. Before his coronation, Saul was considered the weakest of his kinsfolk. This left him in a compromising position. God chose him to be the king over His chosen people Israel. Instead of pleasing the Father, Saul chose to satisfy the folks from his tribe. The Prophet Samuel informed him that God had rejected him and chosen another king because of his disobedience. The news disheartened King Saul. When the Lord's Spirit departed from Saul, he was afflicted by an evil spirit that taunted his mind. He was restless and powerless against it. No person or thing could comfort him. Since God's presence had left him, Saul felt empty within. Yet, he didn't seek God's forgiveness. Some of his officials knew the king was greatly tormented; they summoned David to play soothing music for him.

Whenever David harmoniously played his music of serenity; the distressed spirit temporarily left Saul. Little did he know that God had chosen this shepherd boy to be the next King of Israel. King Saul's throne would be taken from him and given to David. After he discovered this information, a revengeful manhunt was on.

Saul's number one mission in life at that time was to kill David by any means necessary. It was all he thought about day and night. However, God's hand was on that young man's life. This is a must-read story. (*1 Samuel 9 consecutive chapters*)

David was a prolific poet. He penned a large percentage of the Book of Psalms. His creative words dripped with thanksgiving and appreciation towards God. Eloquently, David depicted how he adored and admired his Heavenly Father. The king's slogan "Praise the Lord" is mentioned throughout the book. David disclosed his heavy burdens which were filled with agony and dread. Those times, he felt abandoned by the Darling of Heaven. Each time, God comforted him and provided reassurance that He was with him. Moreover, David shared how destructive and deceptive his enemies and foes were. Their clandestine snares set against his life displayed their ruthlessness. Many times, he expressed how God protected and rescued him from their wicked assails. The Lord was his buckler, hiding place and strong tower. David provided details about his own imperfections. I loved his heartfelt apologies given unto God. Even as of today, the Book of Psalms is treasured and valued by many people.

David was a skillful warrior. He was the type of fighter who you would not want to get into a brawl with. King David had an elite army at his disposal. His mighty guardsmen had their own gifts and talents. They were powerful strategists who were loyal and dedicated to fight until the end. With God on his side, David and his army had an incredible war record. The king successfully defeated his enemies. Because his opponents fought against an invisible force, Jehovah Sabaoth - The Lord of Hosts.

David was a man who faced plenty of challenges. Although the king won many victories, he still experienced times of loss and sorrows. King David became weary and almost wanted to succumb to the ominous pressures of life. New trials as well as his own idiosyncrasies overwhelmed him with excruciating pain. There is nothing like being confronted by an unfortunate situation only to be concurrently bombarded by additional ones. Nevertheless, he was able to muster up enough strength to trust in God.

Psalm 27:13-14, it reads, "I would have lost heart, unless I had believed that I would see the goodness of the LORD in the land of the living. Wait on the LORD; Be of good courage, And He shall strengthen your heart; Wait, I say, on the Lord."

The enemy of our souls is very cunning; he does not love any of us. He especially doesn't love the children of God. He comes even harder against us. We are not to fear him. Because, our God is the King of kings and Lord of lords. The Holy Bible describes the enemy as being the prince of the air. We all know that a king is higher in status than a prince. God owns the Earth, universe, and beyond. Therefore, the devil is a defeated foe. Keep him where he belongs, under your feet.

David wrote about a special location where his enemies did not have access to. It is called "the secret place of God." It is not a natural but a spiritual dwelling place. A place where the intangible presence of God is felt and sensed in a very tangible way. A place where the goodness of the Lord is displayed. A place where love and peace reign. A place where there are no strings attached. A place where freedom permeates the atmosphere. A place where time stands still. A place where exceedingly and unexplainable joy exists. A place where there is no worry or doubt. A place where God's majestic voice whispers into your ears. A place where God profusely equips and qualifies with exhortation and strength.

David's personal stories of struggles and victories are noteworthy examples. God set His approval upon the king's life, and he did phenomenal things. He promised King David an everlasting spiritual dynasty that would be established and endure forever. *(2 Samuel 7:16)* Mary, the mother of Christ Jesus, was a descendant of Judah. She was chosen by God as a vessel to bring forth His only begotten Son, Christ Jesus into the Earth. He is the Savior of the world, and His Kingdom will never end! God's oath was fulfilled. David is recorded as one of the greatest and successful kings in the history of Israel.

Early one morning after spending quality time with the Lord, the Holy Spirit of God (His power and presence) prompted me to open my balcony's vertical blinds. As I rose from my comfortable red sofa to do as I was commanded, I reached for the Holy Bible. For some reason, I knew I did not need it, so I left it on my coffee table. I opened my blinds and moved one of the dining room chairs closer to my balcony's window and sat down. In quietness, I gaped at the remarkable view of the heavens. Abruptly, I spoke these words into the atmosphere of my home:

"The heavens declare the glory of God;
And the firmament shows His handiwork.

Day unto day utters speech,
and night unto night reveals knowledge.

There is no speech nor language
Where their voice is not heard.

Their line has gone out through all the earth,
and their words to the end of the world.

In them He has set a tabernacle for the sun,
which is like a bridegroom coming out of his chamber,
and rejoices like a strong man to run its race.

Its rising is from one end of heaven,
and its circuit to the other end;
And there is nothing hidden from its heat

The law of the LORD is perfect, converting the soul;
The testimony of the LORD is sure, making wise the simple;
The statutes of the LORD are right, rejoicing the heart;
The commandment of the LORD is pure, enlightening the eyes;
The fear of the LORD is clean, enduring forever;
The judgments of the LORD are true and righteous altogether.

More to be desired are they than gold, Yea, than much fine gold;
Sweeter also than honey and the honeycomb

Moreover, by them Your servant is warned,
And in keeping them there is great reward.
Who can understand his errors?
Cleanse me from secret faults.

Keep back Your servant also from presumptuous sins;
Let them not have dominion over me.
Then, I shall be blameless,
And I shall be innocent of great transgression.

Let the words of my mouth and the meditation of my heart
Be acceptable in Your sight, O LORD,
my strength and my Redeemer.

(Psalm 19)

After I recited the above-mentioned passage, the previous quietness saturated the room where I sat. I continued to look up at the heavens. Then, I witnessed a spectacular sight right before my eyes – a sunrise! Wow, the assorted colors from the sun's rays were breathtaking, aesthetic and majestic. Instantly, I praised the Holy Spirit of God for what His beautiful hands had created. Silently, the heavenly hosts are profoundly speaking His inextinguishable love language.

One day at work a co-worker and I were talking about the awesomeness of God and His creation. We walked over to a large picture window and looked outside. It was a crisp winter day with a beautiful blue sky. I said, "look how beautiful it is." With a smile on her face, she nodded and agreed. We stared and commented about its vastness. Its presence is everywhere within the Earth. It symbolizes His endless love, grace, mercy, protection, provision, and hope. It is a constant reminder of the capacity of the Father's incomprehensible power. She and I both thanked and praised the Lord. Truly, the fullness of God is omnipresent.

Scientists are at awe and curious about the magnificence of His creation. Even the ones who don't believe His fingers created it. Certainly, He has revealed intellectual scientific discoveries to them about His universe. However, they have not mastered all details about it. Honestly, they never will. Because the entire secret of its functionality belongs to Him, and the Almighty God chooses what He wants them to know. You must agree – nobody can do it like Father God. *But He is unique, and who can make Him change? And whatever His soul desires, that He does. (Job 23:13)*

When was the last time you spent quality time gazing at the Heavens and expressing your gratitude to the Ancient of Days (a description of God) for creating them? It is beneficial to listen closely to the silence that leads to the revelatory insights of the Almighty God.

Fulfillment of Scriptures

For the word of God is alive and active. Sharper than any double-edged sword, it penetrates even to dividing soul and spirit, joints and marrow; it judges the thoughts and attitudes of the heart. Nothing in all creation is hidden from God's sight. Everything is uncovered and laid bare before the eyes of him to whom we must give account. (Hebrews 4:12-13)

The Word of God is alive and active. All scriptures are God breathed and inspired. He is constantly and expressly talking to each of us every day. All who love Him, hears and knows His voice. He is great, and there is no place or thing that is big enough to contain Him. Yet, He desires to be found by all humans.

Words spoken by God are authentic and laced with power. They flow out of His mouth with accuracy and authority. If He says something, it must come to fruition. He spoke, and it was done. He commanded, and it stood still. There is nothing that can hinder His Word from doing exactly what pleases Himself. He alone spoke the universe and beyond into existence, and there is nowhere on Earth that His Word is absent from. He knows all, sees all, and is all.

Every living person and thing was created and molded by His hands. He knows the full extent of each person's life. There is no part of us that His Word can't reach or touch - spirit, soul and body. He is familiar with every inch of who we are. Nothing is hidden from His sight or sphere. He knows all thoughts before they enter the mind. He is the lawgiver and the judge of the entire world. He is the fullness of righteousness. *(John 1:1-16)*

I love, respect and honor God's sacred scriptures. God said that He would give us the desires of our heart. One of my desires was to know Him through His Holy word. Therefore, I petitioned the Lord to help me memorize scriptures. I knew that they would provide spiritual growth and victory over sin. God granted my request. He gave me the precious gift of scripture memorization. The supernatural ability to remember large volumes of scriptures. I was not able to only hear the words but to internalize them. Equally important, I applied them to my daily life.

I recalled the first day that I discovered that I had the ability to retain and quote scriptures. It was during one of my alone times with Him. I verbalized passages of scriptures for a while. They kept coming from within me. Then, I abruptly stopped talking. I looked at the clock and noticed that I had been quoting them for an hour. Yet, I knew I could continue to say more of them. It was a humbling and amazing moment. They were flowing out of my heart like rivers of living water. Until this day, my soul hungers and thirsts for them. I asked, and it was given. I sought and found. I knocked; and the door was opened.

The Holy Bible holds my interest more than any book on the Earth. Although, I was busy with family obligations and life itself; I made time to read it. One of my favorite places to read was at the neighborhood Borders Bookstore (no longer in existence). I visited the store as much as possible. Its family-oriented environment was comfortable. Their cozy little café served a variety of coffee and tea, light meals and tasty desserts. Some of the employees and I became acquainted. They knew exactly what I wanted to drink "green tea latte." There were other recurring customers who visited the café . There were times when I chatted with them. We respected the silent goal "to avoid excessive talking for the purpose of reading." Other folks played games or met friends and loved ones for drinks and snacks. Their laughter and conversations didn't cause me to lose focus.

At the bookstore, I enjoyed reading Christian books and a large portion of my time was spent reading the Holy Bible. I read it for hours, because I had a hunger for the words of God. Like my physical body needed food – my soul needed the nourishment that came from the scriptures. *Man should not live by bread alone, but by every word that comes from the mouth of God. (Matthew 4:4)*

I had a chance to witness to people, for they were curious about Christ Jesus. I had a chance to pray with them. When some Christians noticed that I was reading the Holy Bible, they smiled and mentioned how much they loved Him too. I have a fond memory of that bookstore. It was a great place to visit. Currently, I spend a lot of time at Barnes and Noble bookstores. If you ask my children or close family members/friends what is one of my favorite places to visit, unanimously they will say "Barnes and Noble." It is a conducive environment for reading.

The Holy Scriptures provide a variety of explanations about God, Christ Jesus, the Holy Spirit, love, creation, mankind, commandments, statues, laws, testimonies, peace, kindness, faith, belief, joy, hope, revelations, knowledge, wisdom, understanding, worship, praise, trust, patience, commitment repentance, justification, sanctification, justice, eternal life, salvation, and so much more. They are applicable to every aspect of our lives. They are never altered by the continuous changing of culture. Through the test of time, the beloved Holy Bible continues to remain the same. It is the most read book in the world. There is no way God created us to not know who He is. It's important to spend quality time reading and meditating on scriptures, for they are an essential requirement for Christian living.

If you are faced with challenging or demanding situations, stay strong against the game of "see-saw." The game of see-saw is to give your cares to God in prayer, and then take them back. It is a continuously up and down cycle. You can avoid it by reflecting on how God brought you through your previous victories.

When waiting on God to answer prayers, be cautious not to implicitly demand or place Him on a time schedule. This will only exacerbate and rattle your nerves. We must not rush the King, but rest with assurance that the Father knows exactly what He is doing. God created time and space for human purposes only. He stands outside of them. They are at His beck and call. They do not have enough capacity to thwart the Almighty God from blessing you. He has perfect timing!

Life can throw some ballistic curve balls at each of us. Thankfully, we do not have to face them alone. Mount Kilimanjaro is a mountain (a giant stratovolcano) located in Tanzania, Africa. Its elevation of height is 19,341 feet. It is the highest mountain in Africa. Because of its height and weight, it's unlikely that a human being or any moving equipment can move it from its location. God can! He moved and placed all the mountains of the earth into their places. His word has the capacity to move or resolve our natural monumental problems too. The invisible God will never forget us. He has our names engraved on the palms of His hands. The body of Christ is the apple of His eye. (*Isaiah 49:16 and Zechariah 2:8*)

Kernels of popcorn are placed into a microwave oven. The hard shells have tiny droplets which surrounds them. As the **heat** from the popcorn becomes steam, it produces pressure on the kernels. When it can't handle the pressure from the heat any longer, the popcorn pops.

Thus says the LORD: *Blessed is the man who trusts in the* LORD, *And whose hope is the* LORD. *For he shall be like a tree planted by the waters, which spreads out its roots by the river, and will not fear when **heat** comes; But its leaf will be green, and will not be anxious in the year of drought, nor will cease from yielding fruit. (Jeremiah 17:7-8)* aka – "God got your back."

It's testimony time - Can I get a witness?

I can attest!! I can attest!! God has been so good to me. Let me tell you! He's been better to me than I've been to my own self. I've been running for God for a mighty long time. I'm not tired yet. This remarkable God answered one of my earnest prayers. You see -- I wanted to experience His manifestations, breakthroughs, and blessings on a continuous basis. I wanted to dwell in the state of wholeness. I knew what it was like to be broken, busted and disgusted. That's not a good place to dwell in. Many of you know exactly what I mean.

I literally drug my past issues around for many years. It nearly wore me out. Listen to me y'all – that extra baggage was burdensome and a noisome. Yet, I kept it fastened and neatly tucked deep down within me. I can say with pure joy that I have been rescued and delivered! My deliverance felt like "cooling waters" from Grandma's well. I was refreshed and rejuvenated! Hallelujah, oh sweet Hallelujah. I was set free by the blood of the Lamb! Now, God is the captain of my ship, and my identity is found in Christ Jesus. Let the church say, "Amen."

Now that's how you make a new sound!

Father, I come to you with a petition. Teach us how to properly love You. Help us to trust and lean on your Word. We will give you all the praises and glory. And it is so, in Christ Jesus' name – Amen.

CHAPTER THREE
WHO ARE YOU?

I have loved you with an everlasting love;
Therefore, I have continued my faithfulness to you.
(Jeremiah 31:3)

My dad was a very laid-back individual. Daddy was kind and generous. Maybe I am a little biased, since I was his only daughter. He treated me like a princess. But seriously, my brothers and I adored him. My dad was very approachable. Two qualities that I loved about him were his patience and listening skills.

He loved his wife and children. Daddy was a diligent worker. Most of the time, he was the sole provider for our family. He had two jobs - a full-time and part-time. His part-time job was not burdensome. He was required to work five days a week/ two-hours per day. Daddy had assistants - my brothers helped him with his part-time job responsibilities. Once in a blue moon, Mama and I assisted them. Occasionally, my mother worked a full-time job. However, she didn't keep jobs for a long period of time. As Mama use to say, "the majority of her former bosses or co-workers were a bit crazy, envious or jealous."

Daddy loved to smile and giggle. He had a great sense of humor. Some of his jokes and stories were hilarious. Daddy kept a big grin on his face as he shared them. Automatically, I smiled before I heard them. As my mama would often say, "Dean, you are so country." This was a derogatory remark against his mannerisms. My daddy was being himself, for it did not take much to make him happy. Although he dropped out of school in the 11th grade, my father was a very knowledgeable man. He was very proficient with the use of his hands. He could fix just about anything around our house. I've never seen anyone count money faster than him. Daddy disliked two things - confrontation and drama. Unfortunately, these two things were unavoidable in our household.

My mother was the boss of our family. In our home, Mama's erratic mood swings set the temperature. They constantly fluctuated. I did my best to stay on her good side. All family celebrations centered around Mama, such as her birthday and Mother's Day. She loved to receive expensive or monetary gifts. One of her favorite questions was, "how much did it cost?" Whenever she received cards, she did not read the words, but grabbed the contents out of it. My father, brothers and I laughed at her gestures. Our birthdays were not as special; my brothers and I did not have birthday parties and rarely received gifts. When we were younger, we received a good amount of Christmas gifts. I believe it was mama's way of making up to us for her inappropriate abuse. Come to think of it, we had to wait until Christmas time for her to be truly happy. Unfortunately, it only lasted for one day, but I was thankful for the gifts.

Mama demanded gifts. She became distant if she didn't receive them. Whenever Mama got mad, we were reprimanded with the silent treatment. My mother would not say a word to the targeted individual or individuals. It is not pleasant to live in a house with a loved one who totally ignores you. This insane form of punishment could last for days. Then, she gradually acknowledged you and would resume conversations. Well, at least during those times of silence we were not degraded.

Whenever she was in a melancholy mood, there appeared to be a thick dark cloud of heaviness which loomed around our house. Unapologetically, her anger was dispatched with hurtful and painful words. Anyone of us could receive the wrath of them. For some reason, she loved to disrespect us in public or during her telephone conversations, especially when she was angry. Her mouth did not have a filter. Indeed, mama spoke what was on her mind. She divulged some of our most embarrassing mishaps with other people. Mama did this right in front of us. Like I said, "no filter at all."

We felt disrespected and unappreciated by her. Let me tell you, if my mother thought one of us said something negative about her to an outside person; she would not hesitate to let us have it. I have said this in a gentle and mild way.

My mama had a strong hand. Whenever she threw shoes at us (my brothers and I), we had to duck quickly. It is amazing how agile we became during those times. My brothers and I received our share of behind whippings. Mama even allowed us to go out front of our house to personally select our own switch from one of the trees. I tried to get the ones with plenty of leaves on them to alleviate the inevitable pain from my behind whipping. To my surprise, mama used to remove the leaves quickly from off the sticks. Boy oh boy, her licks were hard, and her piercing language was hurtful and disgraceful. Mama would fuss and frown her face as she unmercifully whacked our behinds.

There were two incidents where I received two horrible behind whippings, both were not my fault. I tried to tell mama what happened, but she refused to listen to me. The first incident involved a female neighbor who accused me of disrespecting her. Instead of mama asking me what truly happened, she automatically believed our neighbor's statement. The second incident involved one of my brother's mishaps. Mama was upset with him about something that he had done. We were outside playing with some of the neighborhood; my brother and I received a word that our mother wanted us to come home. When we opened the front door, mama dashed out from behind it; she caught us completely off guard. Then, she fussed and whipped us with an extension cord. We cried out for mercy.

As soon as I was able to escape, I ran up the stairs into my bedroom and closed the door. I was convinced that mama was a mean and uncaring person. I was upset because I didn't do anything wrong to be disciplined in such a harsh manner. The cord produced marks on certain parts of my body. They stung and caused great pain. I cried and drifted into a deep sleep.

When my father whipped me, they were light hits and few strokes. I can hold up one hand to count how many behind whippings I received from him. One thing for sure, my daddy did not allow my mother to continue to physically abuse us with extension cords. However, he did not stop her from mentally and verbally abusing us. Daddy was a battered husband. He needed protection from mama. I knew my father wanted to leave my mother. He told me that he stayed with her because of his children. He never wanted to live separately from us.

After he married my mother, he saw that she was emotionally unbalanced. He thought about divorcing her many times. However, his parents raised him to live by moral principles. He decided to remain in the relationship. Moreover, he wanted to help raise Duncan. My father had adopted and vowed to take care of the little fellow. Although my oldest brother was not his biological son, daddy loved and treated him as his own. Whenever someone asked him how many sons he had, my father quickly replied, "three boys." He was a decent man.

My parents were rendered differently. Both were from a two-parent household. My maternal grandparents had eight children, and my paternal grandparents had thirteen children. Yes, you heard me 13 children. My dad shared positive stories of how much his parents loved each other and their children. They were a close-knit family. He grew up on a farm in the back woods of Tarheel, North Carolina.

He had fond memories about what it was like to live on a farm and other childhood experiences. He loved his extended family. I thought it was great how much he loved his parents. Whenever he talked about my grandparents, a sparkle appeared in his eyes and a smile came upon his face. We sat and talked for hours about his fond childhood memories. For some reason, I could not rationalize my dad as a young child, teen, and young adult.

We would constantly hear disconcerted comments against my paternal grandmother. Mama was not happy with her. She said that my grandmother did not accept her because she had a child out of wedlock and a beautiful body figure. Eventually, Mama hindered us from visiting our paternal grandparents and other family members. In our household, we knew how badly she disliked most of my father's family members. It was draining.

Please hear me, 365 days out of a year mama criticized and talked about most people outside of our family. I got tired of her negative perspective of how she viewed them. Her comments were, "They didn't do this for me or that for me." It was never, "Twinkles how do you feel? What was your day like?" No, she always had someone new to talk about. I felt sorry for my father. Heck, I felt sorry for myself.

Mama was an extremely negative and controlling person. At times, I had to walk on egg shells. Everyone else was wrong, and she was always right. People who were not part of our immediate family got to experience a different side of her. Mama treated them better than her own family. She was helpful and respectful to them, and she was very supportive. Her public image was highly significant to her. Inside her home, most times it was not a fun place to be. Outside things were picture perfect.

Some people might comment and say, "that's not the Dot (my mother's nickname) I knew." God bare witness, I am telling the truth. I lived with her. I saw the real deal. I suffered from her blows for many years.

One of my younger adult friends told me that my mother controlled me. I knew it, but I desperately wanted my mama's approval. Believe it or not I didn't bring many of my friends to meet her. I can hold one hand up and count how many of them were introduced to mama. I was afraid and embarrassed of her negative words against me. I did as much as I could not to allow others to hear how she brazenly disrespected her daughter. My mother's unpredictable ways intimidated me. My dad and I were her main two targets.

Mama described her childhood as dysfunctional. She grew up in Rock Hill, South Carolina. My mother hated her father with a passion. Sadly, they never connected. All information about him was totally negative. I heard all sorts of disturbing stories about him. My mother said, "He showed a lack of attention and affection towards me." She said that her sisters were treated better than she was. Also, she hated how he was unfaithful to my grandmother and produced children with some of his mistresses.

My mother had some positive and negative things to say about her mother. Mama said on many occasions how Mother (a name my grandmother's children, grandchildren and in-laws had referred to her as) irritated her. Imagine that, my mother got agitated by her mama. One day I witnessed a car conversation, which included my mother and grandmother. Mama shared some personal information with my grandmother, and my grandmother said it was not true. Then, Mother took over the conversation and talked above her daughter's voice. I watched how Mother antagonized my mama. I shook my head in disbelief. The information that mama shared was accurate.

Mama became frantic, but she dared not to disrespect her mother. Later, she shared the occurrence with my father. She felt disrespected by her mother's negative behavior towards her. Daddy advised her to let her mother know how she felt. My mother said, "Why should I? She won't listen to me." I thought – "hmm that sounds familiar."

One of my mother's biggest complaints was the responsibility that was placed on her to babysit her seven siblings. She disliked this task. Mama said, her father went one way and her mother went the other way. Then, she was left with the chore of taking care of their children. She thought this was too much of a burden to place on a young girl. Some of my maternal relatives said my mama was mean to her siblings and often whipped them. She was thought of as a mean and evil person. On a brighter note, Mama loved and had fond memories about her maternal grandmother and some of her aunts.

At the tender age of 16, my mother met an older guy at a party, and they were attracted to each other. Eventually, she became pregnant by him. This man was much older than she was, and he was married with lots of children. Now, my mom was born in 1942, so I can only imagine the ridicule she faced as a pregnant unwed teenager. The older man abandoned her and their unborn child. This was a devastating blow to my mother. She was ashamed and felt rejected. Honestly, I really think my mother was traumatized by this situation. She had no one to lean on for mental support. Alone, mama gave birth and had a son. The baby was my brother Duncan. After his birth, he was greatly loved and well taken care of by her family.

I did not find out about her pregnancy until I was 16 years old. I did not want to believe it. She never mentioned anything about it to me. I was totally shocked about her teen pregnancy. I felt as her daughter she should have shared this information with me. As an adult, I know this was a delicate situation for her. When I got enough nerve to ask her about the pregnancy, she looked at me and became quiet. She was in deep thought. Then, she said in a defensive tone – "Make sure you don't get pregnant." Her response was incredulous. This was the extent of our conversation – no further explanation. My mom never spilled another word to me about her teen pregnancy.

My father was oblivious to most of the details pertaining to this topic. I sought insight from other extended family members. Likewise, they did not divulge much information about it. This was a bizarre enigma. Remember when I said that my mother was elated that I graduated from high school without getting pregnant, it was her indirect way of saying I want better for my daughter.

I wish I could have learned more about some of the positive things from my mom's past life. All I saw was a woman who was conflicted in her mind. At times, I felt she didn't like me. Her rude behavior made me dislike her. However, deep within me, I loved her.

One day, when I was 15 or 16 years old, my dad and I were having a jovial conversation at the dining room table. He shared information about one of his comical childhood memories. We laughed out loud. I asked him many questions about what his parents thought and other people's reactions about the incident. In my mind, I can vividly see him smiling.

My mother walked into the room with a disapproved look upon her face. She said, "If someone heard you guys, he or she would believe you were boyfriend and girlfriend." I was dumbfounded. Did she imply that someone would think that my daddy and I had an inappropriate relationship based on a conversation? How sick is she?! That's unbelievable.

The atmosphere in the room abruptly changed from jovial to repulsive. Our happy conversation was over. My dad shook his head and silently walked out of the room. I was too hurt to move from the table. I sat there for a few extra seconds. Then, I left the room in disbelief. Her words went down into the very core of my being. They were like knives thrown at my heart. Honestly, I don't think my parents really knew how much that wounded me. My mother didn't care, and my father avoided yet another confrontation.

Behind closed doors, I am sure daddy tried to calm mama down. However, her voice overpowered his. She disrespected and degraded my dad. Mama called him various hurtful names, criticized his mannerisms and broken English. During times of heated arguments, my mother had to have the last word. Daddy walked out of the room, and mama continued to say unpleasant things behind his back. We watched and listened as she insulted our father. She did not care. No child enjoys listening to their parents' quarrels.

Mama was disappointed because of their lack of finances. She thought my dad and his mother had given her some kind of bad luck. She talked about one of her former boyfriends who had financial means. She thought her life would have been better with him. Maybe if she had kept a consistent job and partnered with her husband, they would have done better financially.

I felt it was my responsibility to protect my daddy from her. I made sure to say kind things to him. I wanted him to know how great I thought he was, and how I appreciated his efforts to support our family. A huge fault of my parents was how they included me in their marital issues. If you are a parent, please listen to me – never allow your children to be included into your marital discussions and disputes. This is a no-no. Don't place this cumbersome burden upon them. My introduction to marriage was based on my parents' broken relationship; my mother's abrasive behavior, and my father's pacifist attitude.

When I started to date, I suffered in the relational area. The broken places within me drew the ones (the men) who experienced problems; with low self-esteem or other psychological issues. We were two halves attempting to make a whole. From the very start of each relationship, I was determined that my boyfriend needed my support. I had to be the one who made him happy. I was going to protect and help him to live a healthier life.

I worked hard to keep the peace even if I was unhappy. I was determined to receive and maintain his love and affections. I thought I needed his validation. How strange – I wanted the person who I was in relationship with to love me, but I did not like or love myself. This is ludicrous. I knew in my mind, I thought or believed that I had offended him in some form of capacity. I always found myself apologizing to him. Most times my boyfriend barely apologized to me. Hurting people, hurt people.

There are two sides to a story. I can't tell his side. However, I certainly can share with you how I was tormented in most of my former broken relationships. I felt that the man was the prize, and that I had nothing of value to offer to him. Everything within the relationship centered around his likes and dislikes. Even though he was disrespectful towards me, I remained faithful to him. My dating relationships were physically and mentally draining. Where did I learn how to function and remain in abusive relationships? I learned from the best – my parents. I watched how miserable they were. Yet, they remained in their unhealthy and unstable relationship for many years. Daddy suffered silently while mama complained.

I followed in the footsteps of my father. I suffered from verbal and mental abuse. I kept my feelings within. I was naïve and passive. I allowed them to say some horrible things to me. Please believe me - their words debilitated me. I felt helpless. God knows

I wanted to escape, but I felt obligated to remain in these unproductive relationships. Did you hear what I just said? I felt obligated. Do you see how twisted my mind was? Those abusive relationships continued for a while. Then, they ended in an emotional downward spiral.

I believed in God. At the age of twelve, I accepted Christ Jesus as my personal Savior. However, I did not allow Him to be the Lord of my life. I went to Him in times of trouble when it was convenient for me. After a break-up or other negative issues, I ran to Him to nurse my wounds. He was faithful and always accepted me back into His loving arms. I acted just like some of the biblical children of Israel in the Holy Bible. I jetted to Him in times of need, and I ran away from Him after I felt safe and secured.

I was not yet strong or mature in my Christian walk. I did love Him. I say this in an honest way -- I lived as a seasonal Christian. I gave God limited time and attention. Therefore, it was easy to turn the men that I dated into little gods. They held my attention, and I made them feel like gods. They were always on my heart and mind. Some of them were clingy; it was fine with me because I felt that I needed them. I craved any kind of attention. It just so happened that most of the attention that I received was negative.

After years of unhealthy dating relationships, I cried unto God. I asked Him to please mend my broken heart. I was deeply wounded. I needed Doctor Jesus to heal me. The Father quieted my spirit and softly whispered the below words into my heart.

"Dear Daughter,

I love you with an Everlasting love! You got my breath in your lungs. You are fearfully and wonderfully made. You are made in My image. You are a part of Me. You are intelligent. You are one of my princesses. You are beautiful internally and externally. You are enriched with unique gifts, talents, and honors. You are very valuable to me. You are the image I had in my mind when I brought your parents together to form you. You are not a loser. You are an original design. No one has ever been you or can be you. You are like a shining star high up in the sky. I told you when I created you, I broke the mold. Daughter, you are very lovely. I am the Lord your God – believe me!"

These words spoke to the deepest places within me which were broken. His love won me. If you are in an unhealthy relationship, whether physically, verbally or mentally, you deserve better. You can do bad all by yourself. You do not need anyone to bring you down in life. There are spiritual professional counselors, pastors, or health specialists who can help you – Don't hide your abusive relationship. You are on this earth to live a productive life. You are not a punching bag or sounding board. You are precious. Also, God wants you to be healed and delivered. He gets no pleasure in watching you live in fear and pain. Love yourself – get out of it.

Father, I pray for the readers who are currently in unhealthy relationships. I ask you to shine your glorious light of hope upon them. LORD, let them know that each of their lives matter. I rebuke the voice of the enemy of their souls which spews out deceptions. I demand every prison wall to fall flat down. God, they have said "I can't do it" for so long. I ask you to supersede these negative thoughts with "yes, I can do it by the strength of the Lord. I will do it." And it is so, in Christ Jesus' name – Amen.

CHAPTER FOUR
GOD KNOWS WHO
YOU ARE!

I have called you by name; you are Mine
(Isaiah 43:1)

Although a lot of my paternal family were Christians, I have no idea who introduced me to God. I just knew from a very young age that He was good. Moreover, He loved me, and I loved Him. Also, I knew that He created everyone and everything in the universe and beyond. He had total control. I loved, believed and admired Him. Whenever I made a mistake or did something wrong, I knew to ask Him for forgiveness.

Although, I knew that He had all power in His hands, I was extremely fearful of the dark. Darkness had such an eerie and gloomy feeling, but daylight was awesome (thank God for the light). Some nights at our house were difficult for me. Most of the lights were turned off, and it was so quiet you could hear a pin drop. Our house had two levels with three upstairs bedrooms and 1 ½ bathrooms. Besides the living and dining rooms, the family room and kitchen were connected to each other. Sometimes, my mother asked me to go to the lower level of our house; to bring something upstairs to her. It seemed like her requests came at the most inconvenient time – at night. Of course, all the downstairs lights were turned off. I pouted for a while. Then, I jetted down those stairs so fast that a person would have thought I was Wonder Woman.

My two brothers, Gerald and Tony, shared a bedroom together, and my room was next to theirs. My oldest brother, Duncan, was no longer living with us. He had moved to Long Island, New York, to reside with our maternal grandparents. There were nights I was abruptly awakened. For some reason, I could not go back to sleep so I laid awake in my bed. After a while, I got tired of staring into the darkness and being afraid. I got up enough nerve to get out of my bed to walk into my brothers' bedroom.

Their room was always dark, so I fumbled my way to Gerald's side of the room. He opened his eyes, unstartled by my presence. Then, he gently pulled back the bottom of his bed cover and motioned for me to lie there. I loved how he invited me into his space. Even though my face was inches away from his feet. This was the same brother who attempted to pull me from the dining room table. He didn't make fun or asked why I came into his room. It was a place of safety and rest.

One night as I laid in my bed, I had a dream. It was not a good dream. I can't tell you what the dream entailed, but I was awakened by an unfamiliar voice. The internal voice told me that I was going to die that day. I was a bit startled. I did not know what to make of the voice and the warning of death, but I believed everything I heard. Then, a total calmness saturated within me. I didn't have an urgency to go into my brothers' room, so I drifted back to sleep.

Early the next morning, I informed my mother about the cryptic words I heard from the strange voice. She didn't say anything, but she looked me straight into my eyes with a baffled look. She knew I was telling the truth. I surmised she thought, "What does a ten-year-old child know about death?" Maybe, she didn't know how to explain death to her child. When, I asked her to fix my hair in two bush balls (afro puffs – a hairstyle from the '70s), mama was distracted by my request. I was very specific how my hair needed to be styled, and Mama honored my hairstyle request.

Later that same day, my parents decided to do some yard work. I walked out of our front door and went over to where they were working. I said, "bye mommie and daddy, I'm getting ready to die." They waved and said "good-bye."

Normally, my parents did not allow me to leave from out of their sight. That day was strange from the initial start. As I walked down my neighborhood block, I saw one of my peers who lived in our neighborhood. She and I walked a short distance to the end of our neighborhood street and turned the corner. The sidewalk led us to another street corner. I stopped at the edge of the curve. I noticed one of my classmates was standing outside the entrance gate of her house. We waved. I decided to cross the street. Then, everything became dark and very quiet.

My parents were busy working in their yard. Then, they heard a loud bloom and screeching tires. Mama instantly knew it was me, so she started to run towards the front gate of our yard. Emotional and hysterical, she said to my father, "that's Twinkles!" Both ran towards the horrible sound. God knows they were not prepared for what they were about to witness. As they turned the corner of our block, they noticed people were everywhere.

As they maneuvered through the crowd of people, they saw their ten year-old daughter's unconscious body lying in the middle of the street. My mother could not control her emotions. My parents moved toward my lifeless body and fell to their knees. Out of desperation, they called my name. I was unresponsive. Some neighbors had placed emergency calls to 911. The ambulance driver and other emergency workers must have broken a lot of rules because they got to me quickly. Sirens and flashing lights filled the street. The paramedics assessed my condition, and they were concerned about my back. By this time, additional people came to see what had occurred. Some of them had children the same age as me and others were familiar with some of my family members. Many of them were deeply concerned because I was unresponsive.

The paramedics gently placed my body onto a gurney and lifted me into the back of the ambulance truck. My mother climbed into the back of the vehicle to ride with me to the hospital. The people quickly moved out of the way. The driver's lights and siren were on, and the truck whisked me off at high speed. My dad decided to go home to lock our house doors. Before coming to the accident scene, they had left them open. Then, he would drive the car and meet us at the hospital. I heard this was a traumatic time for him. All he knew was an ambulance left the scene with his baby girl in serious condition and unconscious. He kept thinking about my lifeless body lying in the street.

My father learned from neighbors who witnessed the incident that a man was driving over the speed limit. Then, the driver lost control of his vehicle. When the man saw me, he quickly attempted to stop his vehicle, but it was too late. The impact from the driver's car knocked my body from off the ground vertically into the air. As my body spiraled downward, my back hit the street hard making the loud boom that my parents heard. The eyewitnesses said, it was difficult to watch. There was nothing anyone could have done to help me. The driver was bewildered.

Meanwhile in the ambulance, something remarkable happened: I woke up. It felt like I had awakened from a deep sleep. I saw a friendly Emergency Medical Technician worker and medical equipment. As I looked at my mother, who was profusely crying. She was relieved that my eyes were open, and I was conscious. I wondered why she was crying. She mentioned that a car had hit me. I said, "I told you that I was going to die today." I knew her mind flashed back to our earlier conversation. She shook her head as she wept softly. At that moment, I was not afraid. I was filled with a mystical peace.

When we arrived at the hospital, I continued to meet friendly doctors, nurses and other hospital personnel. After extensive testing, I was moved into a hospital room. My parents were physically, emotionally and mentally drained, but they were thankful to God that their daughter was alive. At the same time, they were concerned about the overall condition of my body. Later, the test results were revealed to my parents. Every test determined that I did not have any head injuries or broken bones. The hospital doctors who were assigned to me were amazed and happy.

My parents decided to go home to get some rest, and then they would come back to the hospital early the next day. My assigned nurse assured them that I would be fine. The nurse came back into my hospital room to check my vital signs. She wanted to make sure that I didn't have pain and if my hospital bed was comfortable. Thereafter, she left the room. I was happy to finally be alone.

I turned towards the hospital's window, and saw that the curtains were left wide open. As I stared out into the starry night, a peculiar thing occurred. Within seconds, I watched the darkness of night quickly fade away. The morning light appeared before my very eyes. I was consciously awake during the entire transition. I rehearsed what I saw within my mind and asked two questions: How could night quickly turn into day within seconds? How could I not get any rest, but it was morning already? This was impossible - I was totally perplexed at what I witnessed with my own eyes. As I laid in that hospital bed, I stared out of the hospital window and thought, "who would believe what I just witnessed?"

The entrance of my nurse distracted me. She greeted me with a pleasant "good morning" and wanted to know how I felt. I pondered if I should tell her what happened. While she was still in my room, my parents arrived early and greeted us. The adults talked among themselves, but I continued to stare at them and wonder if I should tell them what I had witnessed. I decided not to. I thought they would not believe me and think that I was crazy. For many years, I held the above-mentioned hospital encounter deep inside of me. I was afraid what people might think or say about it. Maybe some would believe, and others would not. However, it did not change what I witnessed with my very own eyes.

Good news! My doctor decided to discharge me one day after a speeding vehicle knocked me unconscious. I miraculously walked out of my hospital room without complications. This was a blessing. My parents asked if I was okay. My body was very sore, but I was alive.

God rebuked death, for it was not my time to leave the Earth. I was covered by the blood of Christ Jesus. He is a miracle worker, promise keeper, burden remover, and a yoke destroyer. He is Jehovah-Rapha - The God who heals. There is nothing too hard for Him. He is the Master at making ways. He is Jehovah-Nissi - The Lord our banner. Years after my childhood traumatic accident, my parents and I did not forget about it. Whenever, I shared certain portions of it with others, mama incorporated additional information. The car accident was a unique experience for us all.

As I approached adulthood, I believed that I was not good enough for God or anyone else. Furthermore, I could not envision how God would use a broken-down person like me. I was the least likely to succeed; the one that others overlooked. The last one to be called to the table. I suffered with low self-esteem, shame, guilt, doubt, fear, frustrations, disappointments, depression, anxiety, and other emotional issues. I was messed up. I wore neediness like a blanket.

My mother was a habitual worrier. As she sat on our couch, pulling at the edges of her hair, she stared off into space as if she was in a deep concentration. I watched and observed her behavior. I wondered why she was a miserable person. Even though Mommie was difficult to live with, my heart went out to her. I did not want her to be sad. Unbeknownst to me, I would suffer in a comparable way.

I believe my mother's unhealthy stress techniques taught me how to handle stress. I too sat in total silence and reasoned within my mind. I had to figure out why things occurred in a certain way. Sometimes, I sat on my couch or laid in my bed for hours staring into space. I stayed quiet for a long period of time. Thank God that He knew when I needed to be rescued out of these occurrences. He snapped me out of my stupor.

For many years, I attempted to alter myself. I hated the sound of my voice. I thought it needed a softer tone. My first name, Daffney, was stigmatized. Especially at work, there were people who disrespected and disliked me for some odd reason. They pronounced my name in such a harsh manner. Oh God, some of them were mean, evil and lacked sympathy. They cared about power, authority, and their own careers. Many of their attacks were mean-spirited and spitefully harmful. They attempted to ruin my reputation with dishonesty. The more I attempted to distance myself from Mama, the more I continued to encounter people who possessed similar kinds of behavioral traits like hers.

Publicly, I was criticized, humiliated, and ostracized. Many of my human errors were blown out of proportion, and addressed with rudeness and harsh ramifications. A nominal number of former co-workers witnessed these unjust occurrences. Due to fear of retaliation, they dared not to comment against my insulters' unprofessional and flippant behavior. Some of them offered distant looks of pity or small talk concerning other matters. I stood before them in misery and listened to their meaningless chatter.

I felt unloved and alone. I had no idea why some folks were cruel and abrasive. This bothered me in the worst kind of way. It caused a lot of shame that increased my low self-esteem and self-abasement. I desperately wanted solace. I thought if I continued to change myself, they would accept, recognize or respect me.

My distorted mind frame to change myself overlapped into my walk as a Christian. I worked hard to receive the Father's love, but He never asked me to. Nobody can be good enough to win God's love or bad enough to make Him stop loving him or her. God's love is authentic. He is not always happy with our behavior. Nevertheless, His love and forgiveness are available to everyone.

I attempted to be perfect at everything, so I set out to become an infallible person. I did this based on my own strength. I became a box checker. I wore myself out. After I failed at being a perfect person, I tried to bribe God into giving me breakthroughs. I dressed in an old-fashioned manner (very plain clothing, no make-up and dull hairstyles), followed strict behavior guidelines, (legalism) and anything else that I thought would make Him happy.

I overexerted myself trying to gain His approval. It was equivalent to how I worked to get my mother's approval. I carried the same rituals and methodologies into winning God's affections and kindness. After feeling unappreciated by the Father, I wanted to get as far away from Him as possible. I blamed God for not granting and performing in the manner I thought He should have. It was my way or the highway. God has a way of letting us know that it's His way or no way. I know my behavior sounds horrible. Thank God for His grace! I praised Him that I didn't denounce Him.

I was tired of being in pain. I was tired of trying to change myself. I was tired of striving for perfection. I was tired of being in rooms full of people and feeling their negative vibes. I was tired of my inadequacy. I was tired of being over-stressed. I was tired of my life. I was tired of being a failure, and I was sick and tired of being sick and tired. My past life was very challenging and overly draining. It took many years to be set free from it. The darkness fought hard to keep me down, but the light of hope lifted me up.

You see, I don't only want God, but I need Him. He keeps my mind stable. We work good together. As I stated in a previous chapter, God is the captain of my ship! I am no longer threatened by those superficial attacks from the enemy. God knows my name, and guess what – He knows your name too.

The Father does not care what kinds of mistakes or negative labels have been given to us by misguided family members, fake friends, overaggressive associates, disrespectful supervisors, cunning co-workers, false images from society, jealous foes or backbiting haters. Why let folks who don't know anything about us determine who we are. The devil is a liar. God knows who we are. He loves us very much. The Father is the source of our lives. He is everything good.

This truly amazes me how He saw our body parts knitted together within our mothers' wombs. God designed our bodies and assigned their functionality. He knew us before we even entered the Earth's atmosphere. The prophet of Israel, Jeremiah, was told by God, *"Before I formed you in the womb I knew you." (Jeremiah 1:5)* The Father chose to elevate Jeremiah as a prophet at the tender age of eight. Now, that's young.

However, God saw the bigger picture. The Prophet's spiritual assignment was to boldly proclaim messages from God about a possible judgement against the children of Israel. If His chosen people repented of their sins, He would not allow them to be placed into exile. This was not an easy task, because they were stiff-necked, rebellious, and disobedient. Moreover, they walked in the dictations of their own evil hearts and lusted after false gods. They refused to honor the commandments of God and rejected His prophet's warnings. Jeremiah, was ridiculed, humiliated, and labeled as an instigator. At times, he wanted to surrender to defeat.

The Prophet attempted not to speak the name of the Father or share His words. However, the powerful words of God were heavy within his heart; they felt like a burning fire shut up in his bones. Jeremiah refused to quit. *(Jeremiah 20:9)* God encouraged and provided him with strength. An uncomfortable prison environment, maligned words, or ominous threats didn't deviate him from fulfilling his mission. God trusted him, and Jeremiah did not disappoint the Heavenly Father.

God knew exactly what each of our destinies were going to be before we were born and the various paths that we would select, good or bad. He knew every detail and situation we would face on the planet Earth. The Holy Spirit eagerly waits to help us win at life.

It is such a blessing to bring our issues to God. Am I saying that it's His sole responsibility to move them out of the way to make our lives easier, and we do not have to participate or put forth any effort? No, it is not God's job alone. However, He can handle those overwhelming and unremovable issues. He wants us to acknowledge Him in every aspect of our lives. Why? Because He wants to be in partnership with us. The Holy Spirit wants to help navigate us through life. He wants us to trust in Him. This is what love looks like.

Together with God, we are a powerhouse team. He doesn't want us to act like robots, but to willingly include Him into our lives. Believe me, you will discover that the guidance given by Christ Jesus is much better than a GPS system. He doesn't get side-tracked by satellites or obstructions. You won't have to worry about technical malfunctions. Every time, He will give you bona fide directions. You see God wants us to have a clear and sound mind. He provides the best advice to us when our minds are free from clutter and confusion. His super and our natural, produce a supernatural force. "God got you!" - He knows who you are.

Father, I take this opportunity to praise your Holy name. Truly, you are good. You want each of us to be filled with the knowledge of your will. Thank you for giving us excellent wisdom and spiritual understanding. Thank you for being our strong tower. God, I ask you to continue to draw and quicken us by your Holy Spirit. And it is so, in Christ Jesus' name - Amen.

CHAPTER FIVE
REST FOR MY SOUL

For I will refresh the weary soul and replenish all who are weak.
(Jeremiah 31:25)

I was single, married and divorced twice. In disbelief, some of you are shaking your heads. Others are saying join the club. There are not too many rational thinking people who get married and hope for a divorce. Certainly, this was not what I desired for my life.

I believe in the foundation of marriage and its principles. God is the designer and manufacturer of "marriage." He knows what is required to make a healthy marriage function accurately. Based on the Holy Bible, marriage is a covenant between God, a husband, and a wife, two souls in agreement brought together with the Father's Spirit in the middle of them. Marriage is a spiritual and moral agreement between God and a married couple. Each person within the union has specific roles and responsibilities. This eliminates selfishness and promotes togetherness. Forgiveness, trust, respect, patience, commitment, and unwavering love are key elements that keep the relationship solid. Devotion to God and to each other are the center piece of a successful marriage.

I am glad that the Father witnessed what occurred within my two marriages, for He knows that I suffered greatly. If I had stayed in my first marriage, my children would have been raised without their mother. Because, I would have been admitted to a mental institution. God knew exactly when to rescue and deliver me from out of my depressive situation. For the purposes of privacy, I decided to change my children's father name to Tim. Tim and I were married at the ages of 19 and 20 years of age. I was one year older than him. We had a small church wedding which consisted of family members and friends.

At the altar with our hands locked together, I stood next to my soon to be husband with a big round belly. I was seven months pregnant, but we were not ashamed of our pregnancy. Because, we had everything figured out about life. Little did we know what laid ahead for us as a young married couple.

After our marriage ceremony, we had a country style reception in the basement of our family church. There was fried chicken, ham, collard greens, green beans, corn, macaroni and cheese, yams, potato salad, other kinds of food, cornbread, rolls, drinks (nonalcoholic), sweet potato pies, and various desserts. We talked, laughed, drank, and ate plenty of delicious food. It was a time of rejoicing. Afterward, we left the church to go to our second reception held at his mother's house. She too had plenty of food, desserts, and drinks (nonalcoholic and alcoholic). People were able to eat, drink, and listen to various kinds of music. Later that evening, surrounded by family members and friends, we opened our wedding gifts. Our wedding gathering continued into the night. We had a very long and full day of celebrating.

A couple of months after our wedding ceremony, Tim and I welcomed our new baby boy into the world. He was beautiful and healthy. We decided to name him Toney DeWayne. Tim stated how proud he was of me for giving him a son, and he wanted to give Toney something that he never had – a dedicated and devoted father. Moreover, he never wanted Toney to feel neglected. Years later, God blessed us with two more children Travis DeWhite and Teron DeWitt. My desire at that time was to be a good wife and mother.

Since I didn't have any good role models, I learned by trial and error. I did my best to serve Tim and the boys. Somewhere along the path, I lost myself.

Unimaginable Afflictions

Tim had kept a secret from me. He was a functioning drug addict. Cocaine was his drug of choice, and it was a very expensive and ugly habit. For years, he hid his excessive drug use from me. The day that I confronted him about being a drug addict, he looked me straight into my eyes and vehemently denied it. He responded as if I constituted a conspiracy against him. He displayed no remorse at all. Then, he quickly left out of our house to get far away from my presence. I was left alone in our home attempting to figure out what now? Hours later, he returned but didn't confess. He acted like nothing had happened. My request was for him to stop using drugs. He did say that things were going to get better. No matter what I did or said, he did not quit using the drugs. All the way around, my boys and I got the short end of the stick. I lived in misery.

Tim lived a double life. He portrayed one thing in private and lived another way in public. One of the worst things is to be married and not be able to trust your spouse. Living life with him was excruciatingly painful and challenging. It felt like being on a scary roller coaster ride without a seat belt on. He was a habitual liar and a thief. His deceptive stories were plausible, and I trusted and accepted every word he said. Because, he was my husband and the father of my children. He vowed to take care of me. His words of encouragement made me feel safe and hopeful. He stated that we were a team. Together we were going to raise our children. Somewhere along the path, our twosome became an onesome. My partner didn't hold up his end of the bargain. The weight of everything was placed on my shoulders.

Tim had a professional job that paid him a good salary. For years, he was able to keep his addiction hidden from his bosses and coworkers. They had no idea about his drug habit. He was a smart person and a smooth talker. I referred to him as a walking Webster's Dictionary. He knew what people wanted to hear, and they gravitated to him. Although funds were extremely low for us, he ate at the best restaurants, traveled, shopped at the most fancy men's clothing stores, and wore expensive cologne. He was very selfish and determined to live a productive life - all by himself. It didn't matter that his wife and children were not included. He worked diligently to serve himself and no one else.

Tim decided to attend evening college classes to enhance his thriving career. He delineated how significant it would be for us. The benefit of it will increase our family income. He wasted no time telling me how insignificant my job was. He thought it was menial compared to his thriving career. I agreed. Therefore, he enrolled and took evening college classes. Because of the drugs, he was not able to obtain a degree.

Tim continued to spend huge portions of his paychecks to support his escalating drug habit. He managed to bring home scraps to pay a nominal amount of our household bills. He wanted our personal business to remain within our household. I agreed to keep his dark secret hidden from other family members and friends. Eventually, some relatives began to hear about our financial troubles. They didn't know the full extent of everything that was happening within our family. That is how Tim wanted it.

I lived under a thick cloud of heaviness. In my world, it was always dark, lonely, and miserable. I did not have time for a social life. I was too busy raising my children. I was not going to be absent from their lives. Most times, it felt like I was a single parent. I carried a lot of the parental and household responsibilities. I borrowed money from my parents and from other associates. I became a beggar who had a full-time job. There were times when I didn't have enough money for lunch. I made sure that the munchkins had their lunch money and worried about myself later. Early the next workday, I searched to find someone that I could borrow lunch money from. I made up excuses to cover my embarrassment. It was very humiliating. On paydays, my small lunch debts became a burden. I barely had the money to repay them.

I wanted to leave him. However, I was afraid that I did not possess the right skills and certainly not enough money to raise three children by myself. One day I was fed-up and called my mother from a telephone booth. I did not want Tim to overhear our conversation. I asked if the children and I could stay at her house for a short while. I was desperate. I was tired and drained. I needed refuge for my soul. My mother listened and refused to allow us to temporarily live with her and my father. Her biggest concern was her decorative house, and what church folks might think or say about me being separated from my husband. My mother turned a deaf ear to my plea for help.

I knew I had put myself into this predicament. However, I had no idea how to escape it. Inwardly, my thoughts were, "Mama, please help me. I need you. I have three small children; I want to give them a better life. I need time to figure some things out and constitute a strategy that will enhance our lives. Please mama, I need you more now than at any other time in my life. My soul mourns within me. I need rest for my soul! Mama, please hear my sincere plea. I am about to lose my mind. I don't have anyone else to rely on. Please help me." After our telephone conversation ended, I knew that I was stuck in my unproductive marriage.

I wanted a healthier marriage. I wanted my children to live in a happy and stable environment. Tim convinced me that one day he was going to make a higher pay salary, and it would catapult us into the trajectory of financial stability. If I left him, I would miss out on a great opportunity. Tim would have said anything to deceive me to stay with him. Constantly, he made me think that he was going to work diligently to be a proactive husband and father. Then, life would get better for us. I believed him, for he was a great deceiver. He had great influence over my mind, because I gave it to him.

I knew that things were bad, but I continued to hope for the best for my family. While Tim spent his money on drugs and whatever else pleased him, my entire paychecks were utilized to catch up as much as possible on the household bills. His costly drug habits placed our family in a horrible predicament. To avoid evictions and disconnection of services, I called and talked to our rental landlords and utility companies' representatives. I asked if I could make payment arrangements. I begged them for leniency. Sometimes, I received it and other times I didn't. Because of Tim's drug habit, we moved, and moved, and moved, and moved, and moved, and moved, and moved, and moved, and moved, and moved, and moved and moved. Each time, he never apologized to me.

My children were transferred to different schools. My heart was greatly perturbed. I longed for stability for them. In between our moves, three different times, my mother allowed us to move in with her and my father. She cared a lot for Tim. Mama explained why she liked and respected him. She mentioned that he was the only one who had listened and consoled her whenever people talked against her.

"Mama, this is the same man who steals from your daughter and grandchildren. This is the same man who your daughter has attempted to escape from. This is the same man who has verbally and mentally abused your daughter." In her distorted mind, this was justifiable for their close friendship. Even though her daughter was suffering from his detrimental insults. One time, he physically abused me. He forcefully grabbed my wrist and twisted it. Oh my

God – it was very, very painful. Tears welled in my eyes, and I released a high pitch crying sound. As I held my wrist, I continued to cry. I had never experienced pain like that before. He caught me off guard, because I wasn't expecting him to harm or hurt me. He saw the fear in my eyes. He didn't apologize but quickly walked out of the room. He never physically attacked me again.

Many times, our telephone service was disconnected. This disturbed me in the worst way, and I was embarrassed. I knew folks called and encountered the disconnection messages. I felt hopeless. At other times, we experienced our electricity being turned off. I strongly disliked when I walked into our home to discover that our electricity was disconnected. There is nothing like turning the light switch on and nothing appears. It disrupted my entire day or night. To prevent my children from seeing their mother crying, I wept internally or in an isolated area of the house. This way they could not hear or see their mother in distress. There was no comfort or apologies from Tim. He was guilty and gave plenty of excuses. I will never forget when he unlawfully entered an abandoned house to get some water for us. This was his way of finding a solution. Yet, he continued to use drugs. He was addicted and enjoyed them.

My mother stated that we could come to her house to get water and fill some large plastic jugs. We drove 35 minutes to my parents' house to fill up water jugs. The ride home was very uncomfortable. However, we made it work. Thank God the electricity was on during those times. When I got home, I poured the water into large cooking pots. Then, I placed and boiled them on the kitchen stove. The water was utilized for the following purposes: wash-ups, clothing, dishes, teeth brushing, and bathroom purposes. In retrospect, it is hard to believe we struggled in that way, but we did.

My children and I wore hand me down clothing from the thrift stores. Some family members sneered and laughed at our garments and shoes, for we did not have the latest name brand items. They had no idea that I had to wash a large portion of our clothing by hand. I did the best with what I had. My children were clean and neat. We could never keep a handle on any of our household bills, that included the car payments and car insurance premiums. We owed thousands of dollars to the Internal Revenue Service. However, Tim continued to smoke his drugs and partied at nightclubs with his friends.

Many times, I woke up in the middle of the night and noticed he was not in our bed. Those nights were dreadful and awkward. I walked through the house searching for him. Even though, I knew he was not there. I peeked out of one of our windows to confirm that our car was gone. Whenever he was "missing in action", I was filled with fear. The tears gingerly flowed from my eyes followed by a pity party. I knew he was out purchasing drugs. I hated that he chose drugs over us.

For years, thoughts rummaged through my mind. Why can't your children and wife mean more than those evil drugs? Why can't you get some professional help? Where are you at? Can I raise my sons on my own? Why can't I give them what they need? Then, my small mindset reminded me how I did not possess the ability nor was I qualified to raise, three, male children on my own. I should not attempt to, because I would fail miserably. Then, I would ask God to please bless my children and me. Please don't forget us. After my thoughts and prayer, I followed a regular ritual and waited for Tim to arrive home. I watched the clock like a hawk. It felt like time moved slowly.

For some reason the darkness outside brought such an unpleasant vibe filled with loneliness. Sorrowfully, I drifted back to sleep. The next morning, he provided some lame excuse. Thereafter, we continued in our vicious cycle. It felt like I was living life from inside of a whirlwind. I was shaken to the very core of my being. I wanted desperately to escape our relentless financial situation. We had no funds in our bank account (except for $5.00), and our credit cards were maxed out. Between the two of us (with three children), we had $5.00 - $20.00 per week. Figuratively speaking, we stole from Peter to pay Paul. (What happens when both Peter and Paul are broke?) My paydays were strenuous and pitiful. I withdrew my entire paycheck from my bank account to attempt to pay those nagging overdue bills. We needed every dime of it. I hated living this way and being confined within the borders of debt.

Fighting against debt was an uphill battle. Tim came up with a suggestion; we needed to file for a bankruptcy. He said it would free us from our current debt and provide additional money. At that point, I thought it was a good solution. I wanted rest for my soul! For real, this was not a pragmatic solution. All he needed to do was to stop purchasing the drugs. Then, we could have worked our way out of debt.

I was burned out; I agreed to the bankruptcy. Unbeknownst to me, that didn't help our finances but caused a lower credit score. We continued to spiral downward. Years later, we filed two additional bankruptcies and experienced three car repossessions. One of our cars was almost paid for. I was happy. I figured we would have extra funds when it was completely paid off. Late one night during his drug escapade, Tim wrecked our only vehicle. Thankfully, he was unharmed. We were left without a vehicle for a short while. This was an additional task added to my truckloads of problems to resolve.

I wanted to purchase quality food for my family. This was an insurmountable task. To avoid embarrassment at the grocery stores, I attempted to have the exact amount of money to purchase each food item that I selected. There were times when I miscalculated. These incidents would always be at the checkout line. Some of the people behind me had irritating looks on their faces expressing no sympathy. This was embarrassing. I concealed my tears as I quickly removed some food items from off the conveyor belt. They were items that we needed, but I could not afford them. Times were so rough, that I had to pawn my wedding ring and a piece of expensive jewelry. I knew the pawn stork clerk had underestimated their value. I needed the money and sold my items at a cheap price. I walked back to my car defeated and dejected. This was not a happy time. Tim knew about these incidents. He continued to spend his money on drugs and other excursions.

I searched and looked through clothing items, coats, and the insides of our living room couches or other places around our home hoping to find some money. Whenever I found a dollar bill, I was excited. The money went towards gas for our vehicle. We had a hard time keeping our automobile filled with gasoline. I remember one time when the car was almost empty. I drove to a gas service station. As I was giving the cashier two dollars, a man behind me gave an additional dollar. I was grateful for his gesture.

I didn't always have the proper feminine hygiene products for my monthly menstrual cycle. I found different methods to address my complications. Another major item that we didn't own for many years was a vacuum cleaner. After each meal, I had to get on my knees to pick up the food particles that our children dropped on the carpet. This consumed a lot of time and energy. Yes, those were dark days. Pressure continued to mount within and upon me. Please keep in mind that I thought there was no way out of my debilitating situation. My thoughts were very low. Therefore, my mind was not able to rise above them. *For as he thinks in his heart, so is he. (Proverbs 23:7)*

It seemed like I was born to suffer in our hideous marriage. I didn't see any way out of my situation. Tim stated how the law would be on his side if I took the children from out of our home. I would be blamed for disrupting their lives. I would be found guilty, and he would be rewarded full custody of them. Well as fate had it, we were on the verge of losing yet another home. My mother's heart was touched by God. She allowed the children and me to come live with her. I was thankful for her generosity. After 16 years of marriage, Tim and I separated. My children and I moved into my parents' basement. I called this chapter of my life my "Egypt" experience (a place of bondage).

For the first time, my children and I were homeless. I had attempted to hold it all together for many years. Nothing was left in my reservoir to give. I was mentally and physically drained. I almost succumbed to my plight, but the boys needed their mother to be strong. They were my incentive to move forward into an obscured future. Although it was my parents' house, my mother continued to let me know that she was the boss. I was at her mercy.

For survival purposes, I reverted to my former childhood behavior. I became servitude to her erratic ways. I did my best to stay on her good side. This was necessary to help keep a temporary roof over our heads. I didn't get a chance to properly heal because my mother's constant harassments reminded me of how much of a failure I was. I jumped out of the frying pan back into the fire. It was the same unpleasant experience.

There were workdays when I received alarming telephone calls from my children. My mother was in our assigned living quarters cleaning. She said disrespectful and degrading remarks about me. Her words offended them. God knows it was painful when she insulted me in front of my children. I must say that our area was not overly in disarray. Mama's outbursts were unnecessary, but they were a part of who she was. I needed her assistance, so I kept quiet and took her assails. This is what I meant by serving her erratic ways. Teron said to me as he patted my shoulders, "Ma, Grandma talks about everyone, but yooooooooooou get it the worst."

Tim wanted us to reconcile. He kept calling and pleading for us to get back together. He wanted to move into my parents' house.

He said that our family could be reunited and everything would be alright. His words meant nothing to me. They were filled with emptiness. I knew that this would be the end of our relationship. It was okay, for I was at peace. There was no condemnation. I did my best to keep our family together. Aimlessly, I begged this man to accept his responsibilities. He did not listen. Now, enough was enough.

There were times when I didn't always accept his telephone calls, or limited them to a few minutes. In front of the children, I did not speak inappropriately about their dad. Why should I disrespect their father? I knew eventually his actions would allow them to see his wrongdoings. When a person walks in truth, he or she doesn't have to force others to recognize it.

The boys were getting older and could observe some of the issues within our family. Toney knew more than the other children. He was glad to be away from his father, because he remembered some of the hardships we endured. Teron and Travis were too young to remember most things we faced. I concealed things from them to the best of my ability. I did let them know partially why we moved to their grandparent's house. Our sons were innocent victims caught up in their parents' drama.

Tim's drug use caused him to lose his job. He didn't have a base anymore. He too became homeless. Prior to losing his job, he purchased a new car. He didn't have the funds to afford it, so he got behind on his car payments. Tim refused to return the vehicle to the car finance company, but he drove and lived in his car with no car insurance and invalid tags. Eventually, the vehicle required maintenance. This is when he abandoned his car and sought living accommodations from different homeless shelters, people and social programs.

Tim's fancy wardrobe had diminished to a couple of suits. He continued to wear them until they became shabby and tattered. I knew that God had set me free. My parents were on one accord with me; they did not invite him to move back into their home. They knew that my mind was finally made up, and the marriage was detrimental to my health. I had enough of Tim's shenanigans and his broken promises. I was looking forward to the next chapter of my life. I thanked God for helping me not to lose my mind and for protecting my body during my tumultuous marriage.

One evening in my parents' basement I had a prolific encounter with the Lord, Christ Jesus. He impressed upon my heart in a profound way. Internally, His Spirit revealed to me that I would one day preach His gospel. I would help other people who were deeply wounded. I thought how could I help other hurting people? How could God utilize me in my current broken state? The Lord revealed these words within my heart, "before you married Tim or had your children, I anointed you to preach my word. Before you were in your mother's womb, I had already called, anointed and ordained you." God's words puzzled me. However, I accepted them. At that point in my life, God knew that I was not fully ready to surrender all to Him. He knew that I had much more to encounter as I continued towards my healing process. He vowed to wait for me. The God of the universe and beyond promised that He would wait for me. This blew my mind.

Our boys needed their father. It was very difficult for them. I really could have used his help financially as well as with their overall welfare. When my children were in their late teens and early twenties, I received a telephone call from their father. Tim apologized and asked for forgiveness. He stated how awful he felt for being mean to me. He continued to share how sorrowful he was for his rude and irresponsible behavior. Then, he wept. As he cried, I held the telephone in my hand tighter. There were many adverse memories that flooded my mind.

I was very still and quiet for seconds as I continued to listen to the father of my children weep profusely. Then I said, "Tim I have already forgiven you for everything." My words gave him some kind of solace. He mentioned that I was a good mother. He knew that our children would be taken care of, and he thanked me for taking care of them. Then, we ended our telephone conversation. Why did I forgive him? No one can walk forward in life if he or she continues to look backwards. As of today, he has not paid any child support payments. It doesn't matter. I had forgiven him for everything. It was very difficult, but my children and I made it.

I almost forgot to share this bit of information with you. I was not liable for that huge Internal Revenue Service debt. During certain times when I was not employed, Tim filed and signed alone. Therefore, I was not held responsible to pay for those years. I owed and paid only a nominal amount of money for the years that I had worked. My Heavenly Papa worked it out.

Father, some readers are going through some difficult situations. By demonstration of your Spirit, release unlimited joy and hope into their minds and hearts. God, I boldly speak a sudden turnaround blessing for each of them. And it is so, in Christ Jesus' name – Amen.

CHAPTER SIX
REACHING HIGHER
HEIGHTS

For I will restore health to you and heal you of your wounds,
says the LORD, because they called you an outcast saying
This is Zion; No one seeks her."
(Jeremiah 30:17)

Before I married Tim, my second former husband, Ned, and I dated when I was in high school. He was my first love. I wrote his name on my school notebooks. On pieces of paper, I drew hearts with his name or both of our names inside of them. Whenever we were together, I got this fuzzy good kind of feeling inside of my belly. I enjoyed his company. If we were not together, we were on the telephone talking to each other. Folks told us how perfect we looked together. We would blush and thank them. We both pledged our love to each other.

Almost a year later, he abruptly broke up with me and dated my so-called girlfriend. It was right before my high school senior prom and graduation. I did not see this curve ball coming towards me. The very so-called friend was one who I shared intimate detailed information about my relationship with him. She and I talked, laughed and giggled about him while talking on the telephone. I didn't know what to think or how to feel. I was totally blindsided by their action. Eventually, I wept. The thought of them together made me sad. I thought she was my friend, but I found out that she wanted him at any cost. It also showed his true colors.

For me, it was rejection all over again. That was a very low period in my life. I really thought we were going to get married and have children. A couple of weeks after our breakup, a mutual, older and seasoned female friend of ours attempted to get us back together. I was told by this person not to be concerned about what he did. The older lady said we belonged together. She suggested that I should fight for my man. Therefore, I decided to call Ned. He was happy to hear my voice. I asked him to come join me at our friend's house. He stated that he was on his way.

I was told by someone who observed him during our telephone conversation that my so-called girlfriend was waiting for him. After our dialog had ended, he walked over and said something to her. Then, he quickly got into his car alone and drove away. When he arrived at our friend's house to a house full of her relatives, he was very happy to see me. Ned was relieved to be there with me. We were given privacy to talk. He told me how he cared for me, and how he wanted our relationship to work. My so-called girlfriend would not be a part of his life if we got back together. I forgave him. Then, we pledged our love once again. Hours later, he drove me home. As we happily walked into my living room, the perplexed look on my mother's face told the story.

Let's just say that my mama had a mouthful of words to say to Ned. She let him have it. Her words exploded like dynamite. She did not appreciate how he broke up with me and dated my so-called girlfriend. He attempted to talk and explain how he felt about me. She was not having it. Ned left out of my house defeated and upset. He was through with my mama. I got up and walked into my bedroom broken and deeply wounded. My mother went about her business as usual. Later the same day, Ned broke up with me for the second time. I was devastated. Mama never asked how I felt.

My mother disliked how some of the church folks whispered and gossiped about our break-up. Her reputation was on the line because appearances meant the world to her. It would have been nice if she and I could have sat down together to discuss how I felt about the break-up. I needed a safe shoulder to lean and cry on. Years later, I found out how Ned's mother felt about us. She thought he cared and spent too much time with me. It took him away from running her errands. Yes, you heard correctly – "her errands."

Ned said that she didn't want us to get back together. The persuasion of influence can be utilized in a negative and positive way. His mother got her wish. Her son broke my teenaged heart. With open arms, his mother welcomed my so-called girlfriend as her son's new girlfriend. I always heard how she liked to choose her sons' girlfriends and wives. Eventually, Ned married my so-called girlfriend. The day of their wedding, I was a bit sad. That was a very long day. I thought for sure, he and I could never be together again.

Life is something. Twenty years later after our break-up, my mother saw Ned at an event. She learned that he was divorced and available. Mama decided to give him my telephone number. When he called me, I was a bit curious about how life had treated him. One telephone conversation led to many other conversations. We developed a new friendship that ultimately led to us getting married. After almost three years, Travis, Teron and I moved out of my parents' basement.

I was wife number three, and he was my second husband. We brought previous debt and heavy loads of pain from our previous relationships. Nevertheless, I thought he was perfect. For a little while, Ned and I lived as a content married couple. He shared how his previous wives disrespected him. Therefore, he demanded total respect from me. He believed that a Christian husband had full say over all the affairs of his household, and his wife must be quiet and obey all the rules. To keep him happy I did as I was told.

I worked over-time to keep him satisfied. I wanted him to know that he could trust me with his heart. Once again, I lost who I was. Did I ever know who I was? Months after we were married, I knew that I had made a huge mistake. I was always the one to apologize. Ned never did. He became emotionally disconnected. He didn't know how to express love. I didn't recognize him. Nevertheless, I asked God to forgive me. I refused to back out of my marriage. I was determined to make it work.

Earlier in our marriage, Ned wanted to provide some of the things that I had hoped for. My biggest desire was to own a house, so we purchased a three-bedroom townhouse. There was a major a issue; our mortgage was at a very high interest rate. We were full of optimism that we could handle the hefty payments. Our house was warm, cozy and spacious. It was decorated beautifully. It was home sweet home. I liked it. Mama was disappointed, as she wanted us to move into a single-family house. While our other family members and friends gave us congratulatory remarks and positive feedback, mama did not. She was distraught that we moved a distance away from her. In an odd way, Ned was a form of protection against my mother's controlling ways.

Although we lived paycheck to paycheck, Ned paid our household bills on time. He did not foolishly squander our money. I didn't have to worry about disconnection or eviction notices. God knows this was a wonderful break. I purchased a new expensive car. I was proud that I accomplished something on my own. I didn't have to depend on my parents or other people. I thought it was a monumental accomplishment. Then, something unfortunate occurred. I lost my job. This was not a good position to be in. We had recently purchased a house and a car. It was scary to think that

I might get behind on paying my bills. However, I found a new job within a week. My new salary was curtailed by thousands of dollars, and my car payments became a burden. It was an unnecessary purchase. It was a want not a need. We attempted to find methods to help alleviate some of our debts. Unsuccessfully, we decided to file for a bankruptcy.

The financial and other marital pressures had begun to build up against us. We were swimming in debt. This is when our relationship started to spiral downward. Ned told me that he didn't love me anymore. His words penetrated deep within my heart. I was stunned by them. In a clandestine way, he began to distant himself and planned an escape route to end our marriage. Things were a bit rocky.

The church that we attended was an hour away. I did not attend every Sunday service with him. It so happened that my new job position was at a local church not far from where we lived. It was a requirement to work on Sundays. However, my co-workers understood why I did not attend every service. The Senior Pastor did not want to bring a wedge between the two of us. Ned was livid about our financial situation and our separate churches. Therefore, I applied for another job. I wanted peace to return to our home.

Everything appeared as if we were moving forward in our marriage, until one cold winter night, he woke me up. He wanted to talk to me and requested that we go into our dining room area. I got out of the bed. I could tell something was wrong. I sat at the head of the table. He looked at me and stated that he was going to leave me. His words were rehearsed. I was shocked and sadness filled every part of my being. I asked him if he had spoken to God. In aloofness, he told me that God didn't have anything to do with his decision. I looked into his unemotional eyes and knew that his decision was final.

I got up from my dining room chair and walked up the stairs. My heart felt like it was broken into fragmented pieces and dread wrapped around me like a blanket. There was such a heaviness in the atmosphere. Once I reached the top of the stairs, I looked in the direction of my children's bedroom. Both were sound asleep, and they had no idea of what just occurred. I went into our bedroom and closed the door.

I was broken, but I lifted my hands unto God and prayed to Him. I didn't say any maligned comments about Ned. I needed a breakthrough expeditiously. Then quietness saturated my room, and Christ Jesus spoke unto my spirit in a gentle way. "Are you ready now? What you had searched for in Tim and Ned was always inside of you." You called those men from out of your own brokenness. I came to set you free. Please let me help you. I love and accept you." I cried and wailed. At that moment when I needed God, He was faithful and did not condemn me.

The answer from God gave me clarification. Because of my own psychological dysfunction, I attracted others who faced similar problems. (Broken people hurt people – Broken calls unto broken). My eyes were enlightened. I wanted God to heal, deliver and set me free. I needed spiritual and natural deliverance. After prayer, I wiped my tears away. My somber mood faded away, and my bedroom turned into a jovial atmosphere. Nobody but God can do this. I made a promise to hold on to His powerful and mighty hand.

Do you remember the prophetic promise that God made to me while living in my parents' basement? The Father said that He would wait for me. During one of the most difficult times in my life, God reminded me about His earlier pledge to help me. I felt the presence of the LORD in a tangible way. I knew that He was with me, and I was not alone in my bedroom. Jehovah Shammah, the Lord who is there rocked me quietly to sleep.

I was awakened in the wee hours of the morning. Ned was lying next to me in our bed. All of the lights were turned off. I had no thoughts about our earlier conversation, and there was no fear at all. My bedroom was very quiet and peaceful. I heard a still small voice. Although it was an internal voice, I heard the words as they entered into my ear. The voice said in a soft whisper, "Do you want to know the heart of God?" I embraced myself, for I wanted to know the heart of God. After a few seconds, I said, "yes, I do." The voice of God said, "Preach my word, so that people can be saved, and snatched from the enemy." A wholesome sensation came over my soul. A few seconds later, I started to cry softly. As I wiped my tears away, the still small voice asked another question. "Will you help me?" Seconds later, I answered and said, "yes Lord, I will help You." *(John 10:27)* I kept this divine encounter inside of me for many years.

The next morning, Ned decided to move out of our bedroom into the basement. This was an embarrassing moment. The boys knew that there was an issue. My first response was to protect them. I let them know some of what was going on. Although Ned was going to leave us, I told them that it was going to be alright. I was determined that we would not have to return to their grandparent's house. In order to keep some order within our home, I continued to perform every household chore.

Months leading up to our separation was difficult. Ned became hateful and very cold toward me. I saw an evil side of him. Regardless of our issues, I wanted him to respect me as a human being. He refused to pay any bills. He stayed a bit longer to save money and to look for a new place to live. He did not care. It was as if he wanted me to fail.

Ned called my children's father, Tim to inform him that he was going to leave me. He made it seem like I was the villain, because I disrespected him and would not follow his rules. He wanted Tim to agree with him and label me as a horrible and insensitive person. Tim dismissed every accusation that Ned said against me. He said, "No, Daffney is a good girl. I messed up."

Tim called my mother to share information about his telephone conversation with Ned. Things got messy. My mother wanted to provide me with full details of their conversation. I did not want to hear it. She asked me not to stop Ned from calling Tim. Mama enjoyed the gossip. I asked Ned to stop calling Tim, and he did. Mama wasn't happy.

Ned continued to say disrespectful things about me to other people. A person who once loved me wanted to harm me. His action went from I love you to I despise you. I was determined not to retaliate or be combative against him. I decided to focus on God's principles and raise my sons. In one last attempt to save our marriage, I suggested that we schedule a marriage counseling appointment with a pastor friend of mine. I knew that this pastor would be impartial.

The pastor listened to both of our stories. I saw how he worked diligently to help us. After a while, he said to Ned, "there is no substantial biblical reason for you to divorce your wife." These words were released into the atmosphere with authority. Ned did not say a word but just stared. I had hope that the godly advice would register with him. When our session was over, Ned stated that he was going to leave me no matter what. I asked, "why do you want to leave me?" He said that he wanted to be free to do as he pleased. I was deeply wounded.

Days later, I spoke to the pastor about the marital counseling session. He said, "Daffney, I have met with married couples for over twenty years. I always was able to get into their hearts. I could not reach Ned's heart. I tried diligently, but it was too cold." The pastor asked me to take care of myself. Pitifully, I nodded my head. I cried and cried for my marriage. Whenever I asked God to help save my marriage, I became depressed. Whenever I accepted that it was over, I became stronger. I needed to walk through my various painful and emotional feelings.

One night as I laid in my bed, tears fell aimlessly from my eyes. I did not want another divorce. Just the mention of it brought sorrow. I cried and wailed for a while. I wondered what was wrong with me – another break-up. Didn't I work hard enough to receive Ned's love? Didn't I work diligently to please him? I afflicted myself with demeaning words. Afterward, I became depressed.

I had hoped Ned would have said, "I love you, and we can make it no matter what. Let's find an inexpensive place and live on a budget until we dig ourselves out of debt." I had decided to climb out of my bed, go downstairs to the basement, and get on my knees to beg him to stay with me. As I attempted to move my feet from off the bed, I abruptly stopped. I could not do it. Instead, I called out to God to help me. The Master of the universe heard my cry. After a while, my fearful thoughts vanished. The Holy Spirit reassured me that I was not to blame for Ned's decision. I had to let him go. If I never received an apology from him, I should not allow it to hinder my life. These words from God comforted me.

From that day forward, Ned and I were of one accord. Both of us wanted out of the marriage. Later, Ned told me that he had met someone else who had more money and was more successful than I was. He wanted me to know how he was going to live a lucrative life without me. Because this person had more than I did, this made her a better woman.

After two years and two months of marriage, Ned moved out of our home, and I was delighted and relieved. Travis said, "Mom I heard you singing praise and worship songs during Ned's evacuation." Indeed, I was. I didn't shed a tear. Subsequently after he moved out, one of my church sisters and I went to breakfast. We had a wonderful and encouraging conversation. While at the restaurant, my telephone rang. It was a call from my daddy.

I knew that he was filled with sorrow because his daughter was faced with yet another life changing situation. Daddy said, "Twinkles, this is not the worst thing that can happen to you. Go forward and live your life." I assured my dad that I was well and had all intention to move forward. After talking to him, my friend and I continued with our conversation. She and I laughed and giggled. I can truly say that I have never missed Ned.

As you may recall before my separation from Ned, I applied for a new job position. Well, it miraculously came through. The company offered excellent benefits and a very decent salary. I started my new position a couple of months after he left me. I asked Ned not to remove my children and me from his health insurance policy. Of course, he did. Although he dropped us from his policy, the next day I was able to get a new health insurance plan that included my sons too. I love how God works things out.

Ned managed to leave me with the responsibilities of our mortgage payments and a truckload of bills. The bulk of our bills was too much to bear. My number one priority was to find a place for us to live. I was determined to keep my vow. We were not going to move back to my parents' house. By faith, I knew that I was going to make it. God was going to help me locate a safe and affordable place to live, and that is exactly what He did.

I shared a portion of what I had gone through with a woman who attended the same church as I did. In return, she called her cousin who was a manager at an apartment complex. The manager called me and introduced herself. She sounded like a very nice person. She had one spacious two-bedroom apartment unit available, and it was located on the third floor. The lady stated that the apartment complex rarely had a two-bedroom available. She scheduled an appointment to meet with me. When I hung up the phone, I was filled with excitement. I knew this was a blessing from God. It was perfect timing. My house was already in the process of foreclosure.

Finally, my appointment date arrived. I went to view the apartment unit. I noticed how the complex was maintained and isolated from a main street. After touring the apartment, I was impressed by the structure and dimension of it. She asked me to complete an application. I mentioned how I was in the process of foreclosure and my credit was not good. After I released these words seconds later, fear gripped me. I waited for her to reject me. She smiled and told me not to worry.

I completed the form and paid for the application fee. The manager told me to go home and pack my belongings. Within days, I got the approval call. I was so happy. A couple of days later, I was given the key to my apartment. The manager smiled and encouraged me. She told me that she believed in me. Her words inspired me. It was a wonderful feeling to hold the lease that displayed my name alone. I had been liberated.

I took Travis to see our new home. As I showed him around the apartment unit, I was filled with enthusiasm. He looked at me in disbelief. He did not catch the vision. He wondered how in the world could we place all of our furniture into a smaller place. After we moved in and got settled, Travis said that he could not fathom how things would be situated, but "Ma, you did it." Never underestimate a determined mother. We were quite comfortable in our new home.

The apartment complex that we moved into had an affordable monthly rental rate. It was in a very quiet neighborhood. The management demanded it. Many of my neighbors had lived there for a long time. Some of them mentioned about the very long waiting list for two-bedroom apartments. They confirmed the words of the property manager.

It might seem like it was unfair how I got pushed to the front of the line. God knew that I had suffered for a very long time. This is not to say that others on the aforementioned list did not have their own personal struggles. We all have seasons when breakthroughs arrive. This was my appointed time to be blessed.

When you pass through the waters, I will be with you; and through the rivers, they shall not overflow you. When you walk through the fire, you shall not be burned, nor shall the flames scorch you. (Isaiah 43:2)

Ned and I lost our home to foreclosure. He filed for a separate bankruptcy which protected and eliminated him from any obligation of our mortgage loan. Therefore, I was held liable for it. I didn't know how I was going to pay it off. I continued to work hard to move forward and raise the boys. Years later due to a technicality, the foreclosure was deemed illegal. The loan was dismissed, and funds were owed back to us. What a victory!

Father, thank you for being God. There is nothing too hard for you. Lord, many of the readers have financial needs or other kinds of necessities. One touch of your finger tip can dispatch unfathomable breakthroughs and miracles. Work it out Lord, our eyes look toward You. And it is so, in Christ Jesus' name – Amen.

CHAPTER SEVEN
WHERE IS THAT
SOUND COMING FROM?

Now the Lord is the Spirit; and
where the Spirit of the Lord is, there is liberty.
(2 Corinthians 3:17)

There are approximately over seven billion people living in our world today. Each of us is headed in a different direction. Every day brings its own unique ups and downs. Although life can be an enigma, many of us are determined to press forward and dig deeper to unravel its hidden mysteries.

One thing is for sure, everyone has a desire to belong and to be accepted. We need genuine love, hope, peace, joy, laughter, and security. There is a God-sized hole inside of everyone. Without Him, no human being, earthly knowledge, or material items can fill this spiritual void. Humanity was created to display the glory of God. Our main priority is to serve Him. We can never have impactful experiences on earth without being in synchronized with His divine presence.

Unattached from God, we are like fish, flip-flopping on dry land in dire need of water. The answer to the world's questions, problems, and directions are found in Christ Jesus. God is the ultimate source who supplies everything pertaining to life and holiness. His Word alone can saturate our God-sized hole with inner freedom.

Freedom in Christ Jesus brings liberation. It allows individuals to remain connected to the source of unfailing love. This kind of freedom allows anyone to know exactly who he or she is. Yes, it teaches us how to live life from the inside out, to thrive in every moment, and to accept life as a gift. It has nothing to do with how much a person acquires. It provides purity of mind and thoughts. Unashamed and unapologetic serenity releases a deeper logical reasoning of one's existence. Peace freely oozes inwardly and outwardly. Freedom fills the spirit, soul, and body with the awareness of His wholeness.

The wholeness of God gives the beauty of satisfaction in its totality. There is nothing lacking within its borders. Whether privately or publicly, it has a strong shield of protection. It brings forth the finer things of life; things which are meaningful and everlasting. It builds a foundation that others admire and long for. Contentment is loaded with wealth, and each part of it is cherished and valuable. Boldness and confidence are ingrained within its court. Wholeness teaches not to minimize the degree of distinctions between small and large accomplishments. Both receive the same measure of enjoyment. Equally as important, it molds the individual to think victoriously while in the trenches of adversities. *Weeping may endure for a night, but joy comes in the morning. (Psalm 30:5)*

Those who possess satisfaction are continuously reminded of God's divine goodness and promises, and an overflowing of knowledge which remind them that all things will work out for their good. The florescent light of wholeness exemplifies the indispensable glory of God.

One day, I was in fervent prayer. I heard the word "Rest." I knew it was something of value that God wanted to convey to me.

This is what He shared with me about the meaning of the word "Rest." May it bless you.

"R" means Relaxation - Believe, rely, and depend on His faithfulness, and acceptance of His ageless wisdom. It is in full control. Fill yourself with His divine words of hopefulness and encouragement. Keep Him as the main source. Never allow the voices and the opinions of the world to overpower His voice. Know without a doubt that He is absolute truth. Whatever God says, do it! Regardless of what is portrayed in the natural, keep your mind and heart stayed on Him. Don't dwell in the realm of frustration and discouragement. Hear, listen, and obey spiritual insights to avoid the invisible pitfalls. Be productive and know that God wants the best for you and never desires evil.

"E" means Elevation - The magnitude of its height literally lifts you high. It crowns one with honor, integrity, and dignity. Exaltation dwells within its borders. At this altitude, it equips you with precision. God shows Himself to you at a higher dimension. The indwelling of the Holy Spirit endows you with the knowledge of God's will. Within your heart, you hear heavenly anointed music playing. It brings forth a perpetual stream of peacefulness.

When you are very still, the LORD allows you to hear conversations between your spirit and His Spirit. Doors of advancement stand at attention. They lead you to a realm of blissful favor. Creativity, witty ideas and inventions, divine dreams, and spiritual enrichments live inside its vast perimeters. Each brings a smidgen of awareness about the Father's capacities. Without hesitation, you know that God is with you.

"S" means Strength - Dunamis power at its finest level. It provides unimaginable energy. Strength catapults the chosen of God into his or her rightful place in all things. Strength moves at an accelerated speed. It is stronger and more sophisticated than any weaponry known unto humanity. The power of the Lord makes you courageous.

The river of our Heavenly Papa has unlimited resources to replenish your spirit, soul, and body at any given moment. The healing waters sprout words of inspiration and encouragement. Effectiveness displays the longevity of being rooted and grounded in the rich soil of God. The strength of the Lord is your joy. Do not place your trust, faith, or hope in other substitutions. They are useless before the mighty hand of the Lord.

"T" means Tenacity - It keeps you overlaid with determination and dedication. It comes from deep within your spirit. It is a supernatural endurance which never ceases. The robustness of it helps you to reach your destiny in a respectful and timely manner. Passionately, it springs forth into the essence of mobilization. Whatever you do, listen carefully to its instructions. God uses tenacity as a tool to help His people to go through difficult trials and tribulations. Sometimes, it directs you to walk at a slower pace. At other times, it tells you to move at a faster speed. Tenacity produces an inner deeper edge of thoroughness and thoughtfulness.

God wants His children to R.E.S.T. Jesus said to come to Him, and He will give you rest. Our God is not a liar, for His absolute trustworthy words have stood throughout the test of time. Rest in Christ Jesus is the recipe for prosperity and success. I ask you to revisit the above-mentioned information pertaining to R.E.S.T.

Mediate upon these scriptures:
Relaxation:

- *And my God will meet all your needs according to the riches of His glory in Christ Jesus. **Philippians 4:19***

- *Come to Me, all who are weary and heavy-laden, and I will give you rest Take My yoke upon you and learn from Me, for*

I am gentle and humble in heart, and you will find rest for your souls. For My yoke is easy and My burden is light. **Matthew 11:28-30**

- *Be anxious for nothing, but in everything by prayer and supplication, with thanksgiving, let your requests be made known to God; and the peace of God, which surpasses all understanding, will guard your hearts and minds through Christ Jesus.* **Philippians 4:6-7**

- *Do not fear [anything], for I am with you; Do not be afraid, for I am your God. I will strengthen you, be assured I will help you; I will certainly take hold of you with My righteous right hand [a hand of justice, of power, of victory, of salvation].* **Isaiah 41:10**

- *Truly my soul finds rest in God; my salvation comes from him. Truly he is my rock and my salvation; he is my fortress, I will never be shaken.* **Psalm 62:1-2**

Elevation:
- *And he brought me up out of the pit of destruction, out of the miry clay, and set my feet upon a rock; he hath established my goings.* **Psalm 40:2**

- *The Lord replied, "My Presence will go with you, and I will give you rest."* **Exodus 33:14**

- *Humble yourselves, therefore, under God's mighty hand, that he may lift you up in due time. Cast all your anxiety on him because he cares for you.* **1 Peter 5:6-7**

- *No one from the east or the west or from the desert can exalt themselves. It is God who judges: He brings one down, he exalts another.* **Psalm 75:6-7**

- *But whoever looks intently into the perfect law that gives freedom and continues in it-not forgetting what they have heard but doing it-they will be blessed in what they do.* **James 1:25**

Strength:

- *And He said to me, "My grace is sufficient for you, for My strength is made perfect in weakness." Therefore, most gladly I will rather boast in my infirmities, that the power of Christ may rest upon me.* **2 Corinthians 12:9**

- *He gives strength to the weary and increases the power of the weak. Even youths grow tired and weary, and young men stumble and fall, but those who hope in the Lord will renew their strength. They will soar on wings like eagles, they will run and not grow weary, they will walk and not be faint.* **Isaiah 40:29-31**

- *The LORD is my strength and song, And He has become my salvation; He is my God, and I will praise Him; My father's God, and I will exalt Him.* **Exodus 15:2**

- *God is our refuge and strength, a very present help in trouble.* **Psalm 46:1**

- *That He will grant you, according to the riches of His glory, to be strengthened with might through His Spirit in the inner man.* **Ephesians 3:16**

Tenacity:

- *And not only this, but we also exult in our tribulations, knowing that tribulation brings about perseverance; and perseverance, proven character; and proven character, hope; and hope does not disappoint, because the love of God has been poured out within our hearts through the Holy*

*Spirit who was given to us. **Romans 5:3-5***

- *Trust in the LORD with all your heart, and lean not on your own understanding; In all your ways acknowledge Him, And He shall direct your paths. **Proverbs 3:5-6***

- *Therefore, do not throw away your confidence, which has a great reward. For you have need of endurance, so that when you have done the will of God you may receive what is promised. **Hebrews 10:35-36***

- *No temptation has overtaken you except what is common to mankind. And God is faithful; he will not let you be tempted beyond what you can bear. But when you are tempted, he will also provide a way out so that you can endure it. **1 Corinthians 10:13***

- *Therefore, my beloved brethren, be steadfast, immovable, always abounding in the work of the Lord, knowing that your labor is not in vain in the Lord. **1 Corinthians 15:58***

From Lack to Fullness

Father God is the potter, and His child is the clay. The Potter places the clay into His bare hands. Then, he tears and pulls it apart. Next, he rolls, presses, and pats the clay. The Potter places it on the spinning wheel to reshape it. No one knows exactly what will become of the clay, but the Potter knows. He gently and carefully applies a certain amount of water onto His hands to massage the clay. He makes sure all the fragmental pieces are fastened and molded together. Before long, it has a brand new form. The Potter moves the vessel to a designated place of total darkness, isolation, and obscurity.

The vessel is in a lonely place. It feels the pressure of its unwelcomed environment, but the Potter is not absentminded. While the clay dries, He watches and guards His priceless possession. When it is thoroughly dried, the vessel is moved from its temporary shelter. He positions the work of art at the center of a beautiful glass mantel. Others are mesmerized by the exquisiteness of His handiwork. The Potter (God) beams as He adores His masterpiece (His child). He knows when His child is pliable and ready to be used for His services.

My Journey to Wholeness

My process to wholeness was long and difficult, and I pursued it with my whole heart. I talked, cried, wailed, whined, and complained to God. During the time of my weakest moments, the Father enveloped me with His unconditional love and overwhelming affections. Let me tell you, God has an endless open door policy. When I was not able to talk to anyone or didn't have a shoulder to lean on, His door was accessible at any time of the day or night. He allowed me to lean and depend on Him. Our encounters didn't make Him faint, nor was He weary. He was faithful. I certainly was not. I slipped and fell along the course, but God did not abandon me. He extended truth, grace, and mercy toward me. God knew when I needed to be comforted and disciplined. His love won me.

I had my own preconceived notion on how to accomplish wholeness. I tried different remedies. At first, I approached it with a formula of steps. I sought the guidance of others and read bestselling books. Some of the information provided by the Christian authors was beneficial. However, I discovered that there were no short cuts to wholesome living without addressing every aspect of my life.

You see, I did not want to confront the issues of my past. I didn't want to endure the pain nor put forth the effort to silence them. I knew that it would be an arduous and strenuous task. I wanted the journey to be easy. I wanted to get rid of my problems by osmosis. I wanted to close my eyes and open them to a magical antidote of wholeness.

Day and night, the war within me continued to rage. I must confess that I impeded my own process of healing. I picked and chose which areas of my life I wanted to surrender to God. I created a beautiful decorative mask. For years, it became my defense mechanism. Finally, I got fed up with my life and the false image that I had formed. I was tired of living in a rut. I became exhausted at playing the leading actress role in my own horror movie. I was tired of being the victim. No more waiting for someone to rescue me.

I decided that enough was enough. By any means necessary, I was going to become a victor. How did I do it? I stopped slipping and sliding, and I repented for my wrong doings. I gave all of myself to Christ Jesus. I placed my hope and trust in Him alone. This changed my life exponentially. I grew in His love and experienced Christ Jesus on a higher level.

God and I formed an intimate relationship. He became my best friend. This allowed me to become familiar with His voice. I applied the Holy scriptures to my daily life. I agreed, believed, and trusted in His principles. I refused to allow my feelings to dictate my thoughts and actions. If I disobeyed His commands, I confessed my sins. The Holy Bible teaches that God forgives those who confess their sins. *(1 John 1:9)* He promised to remove our transgressions as far as the east is from the west, never again to remember them. *(Psalm 103:12)*

With the help of the Holy Spirit, I did not allow any of the enemy's tactics to impede my progress toward wholeness. I did not allow thoughts of condemnation to seep into my wealthy place in God. My mind was focused on Christ Jesus.

I spoke words of faith into my atmosphere. Whether silently or verbally, the sound of them ricocheted and brought calmness to my soul. I was inundated with His encouragement and inspiration. He gave me rest, quietness, and confidence. My soul was nursed back to health. I received the blessing of the Lord, the goodness of who He is. No longer did I envision myself as being unimportant. God is blessed, and He certainly doesn't have insignificant children. The devil is a liar.

I became acquainted with myself. Things I liked and disliked were reevaluated. However, there were unanswered questions pertaining to my unhealthy past. Why did it cause me to make the wrong choices? Why did I need to be accepted at any cost? To get answers to my questions, I needed to return back to my childhood. The place where I didn't want to go. Finally, I was ready to face my past. The Holy Spirit revealed some unknown mysteries about the dynamics of my family history. Confirmations came from kinfolk much older than me. This allowed me to know that I was heading in the right direction.

After a while, I discovered why I had a dire need for acceptance. The lack of my mother's love, attention, and approval impacted me in a negative way. For a very long time, I did not address the hurt or share any aspects of my painful and abusive childhood with anyone. It didn't help that I chose to ignore it. The pain was suppressed into my subliminal mind. This kept the door open to fear, rejection, depression, unworthiness, and loneliness. The unpleasant spirit of loneliness deprived me of peace and told me that I was indifferent. For many years, these strongholds literally controlled and dictated my behavior from childhood to adulthood. They caused a detrimental effect in every area of my life. Most of my decisions were based upon them. Unconsciously, I was a prisoner to my destructive emotions.

I had to go deeper into the wounded struggles from my childhood. Since I could not physically go back to my past, the Holy Spirit revealed much information by divine visitations, revelations, and insights. At times, some images from my past were very scary and painful. Some nights I wept as I laid in my bed. However, I did not run away from them. I wanted to be healed. Each unresolved issue that was disclosed to me needed to be addressed. Gradually, one layer at a time led me closer to my deliverance. His perfect love eradicated the tormenting of my mind. Where fear reigned, faith replaced it. Christ Jesus became more real than any of my issues. His divine peace flowed like a river. It was an awesome experience.

I started to make healthier choices. God showed me a new way of living. I didn't allow my dead past to control my life anymore. It only had the power that I gave to it. When negative thoughts attempted to arise in my mind, I went to war. Through the power of the Holy Spirit, I starved and suffocated those thoughts. I used the name above all names. The name which makes all strongholds bow down. I called on the name of "Jesus." There is power and authority in His name! Heaven had my voice on speed dial. Every time I called on His great name, I received power to keep moving forward. Relentlessly, I loaded my mind with words of faith and affirmations. I spoke them into the atmosphere. The word of God teaches us to decree a thing, and it shall be established unto us.

Consistency and personal boundaries were formed and kept. What I said matched what I did. I became disciplined. My "yes" was yes and my "no" was no. I did not ponder about the unknown things and what people negatively thought about me. I stopped being my worst critic. With the help of God, I silenced the voice of my enemy. I put forth more effort to guard my heart and held tightly to things that were helpful and healthier for me. God had an awesome plan for my life which didn't consist of brokenness, depression, and anxiety. I am happy to report that my broken past is no longer in charge of me. Now, I live and operate in the newness of Christ Jesus.

Where is that sound coming from? Oh that's Daffney Miché Hawkins walking and thriving in freedom, wholeness, and rest!

Father, I ask you to bless every reader with your divine REST. From the crown of their heads to the soles of their feet. There is an abundance of peace which flows from your divine presence. Release your perfect love and peace into the atmosphere. God, thank you for rewarding us with your goodness. Without you, we are nothing. And it is so, in Christ Jesus' name – Amen.

CHAPTER EIGHT
VICTORIOUS LIVING IN
CHRIST JESUS

*Any man who is in Christ Jesus is
a new creation; old things have passed away;
behold, all things have become new.
(2 Corinthians 5:17)*

Christ Jesus is my Promise Keeper.

Christ Jesus is my Way Maker.

Christ Jesus is my Comforter.

Christ Jesus is my Healer.

Christ Jesus is my Strong Tower.

Christ Jesus is my Provider.

Christ Jesus is my Protector.

Christ Jesus is my Mountain Mover.

Christ Jesus is my Sustainer.

Christ Jesus is my Everything! Let everything that has breath praise the Lord! The Lord is mighty awesome, and He is worthy to be praised. Praise the Lord in singing, clapping, dancing, and rejoicing. If I had ten thousand tongues, I still could not express my thanks to Him for His goodness. God is very good to me. Even when I was not good to myself. He took my mess and turned it into a message. Literally, God is in a class all by Himself.

There is not a nanosecond which passes by that someone is not lifting his or her hands to revere His Holy name. Yes, God is the Great I AM that I AM. The one who created the heavens and earth. The Master of the universe and beyond. He holds all of the bodies of waters in the hollow of His hand. He measures the heavens with a span. He knows the exact amount of people living on earth. He weighs the mountains on the scales and the hills in a balance. No one directs, instructs, or counsels Him. God sits above the circle of the Earth, and we are like grasshoppers in His sight. (*Isaiah 40:12-15, 22*) He is all that ...and a bag of chips....with dip (onion flavored), and a drink, with a straw inside of the cup.

If you are faced with a trial or tribulation, lift your hands up high and say to the Lord, "I trust you." Although your problem(s) may not be resolved, I want you to outwardly say these simple words by faith. "God, I thank you for how you *worked* my situation(s) out. You are the captain of my ship. I know that you are able. You won't lie, for You are the immutable God. I will continue to stand on your holy words and promises. I already believe and know that I have the victory."

A word of warning – Be careful not to get stuck in the "why me?" questions. The enemy of our soul is full of deceptions, and he wants to immobilize us through our unanswered questions. There are many people who can't move forward because of his subtle attacks. They desperately want full explanations of the "why me?" questions. "Why did I have to face these issues while others didn't?" They are mad and disappointed at God, because He didn't reveal prominent details and facts concerning their circumstances. They are angry at the only source who can truly help them.

If God chooses to reveal the "why me?" questions, the information is needed for a greater cause. It's meant to be a blessing not only for you but for others too. If He chooses not to reveal the "why me?" questions, God doesn't want you to become stagnate and lose heart. Maybe, you were not able to bear the details at that particular season in your life. It is not to say that you will never discover His reasoning. The Almighty wants you to trust in His decisions. God is the righteous judge. He expects us to wait quietly and patiently on Him. When a person waits quietly and patiently on God, there is not a consistent uneasiness. This is when your feet are planted on solid ground. It has nothing to do with your strength and capacity. It's a God thang. It's an inner spiritual calmness which propels you to hold on. There is an available reservoir of expectations that penetrates through every fiber of your being to believe, hope, know, understand, and trust in Him. Against all odds, you know that you know, that you know, that you will come through your trials triumphantly. Godly patience seals your eyes on Christ Jesus.

The Center of God's Heart

One night in the wee hours of the morning, I was awakened by God. I laid in my comfortable bed snuggled under my amazingly warm and plush blanket. I was reminded about a mother and daughter's poignant interactions. While at church, I witnessed a heart-warming encounter. It was a tear-jerker moment. I sat and admired how the mother catered to her adorable baby girl. Her daughter was about nine or ten months of age. They admirably looked quietly into each other eyes with pure love. As the mother began to talk to her daughter, I noticed the baby was very attentive to her mother's every spoken word. I loved how they looked into each other eyes. No amount of noise distracted their conversation.

They smiled and laughed. They were in their own unique little world.

Abruptly, the mother said to her baby "I forgot to give you something." She stepped away to get something from her daughter's diaper bag. I watched how the little girl's face was filled with expectation, for mama was doing something special for her. The mother returned with a big smile planted on her face. There was a yummy snack in one of her hands. Her daughter was filled with joy as she grabbed the snack out of her mother's hand. There was a delightful beam of light that filled the eyes of the little girl. The mother watched as her daughter happily rocked backward and forward chewing her snack. They continued to gape into each other eyes.

Christ Jesus' love is genuinely good. He is forever faithful and committed to His children. It doesn't matter what you have said or done. His unconditional love will never dwindle away. The above-mentioned story is a wonderful illustration of God's love. He sees us through eyes of love. We are on His mind day and night. His care and kindness are beyond measure. God knows exactly how to put a smile upon our face. As the baby waited for her mama with full expectation, the child was not disappointed.

Have you encountered the awesome reckless love of Christ Jesus? It is always readily available to everyone. The Father loves you. He invites you to come closer to Him.

I love this passage of scriptures:

Because he has set his love upon Me, therefore, I will deliver him;
I will set him on high, because he, has known My name.
He shall call to Me, and I will answer him;
I will be with him in trouble; I will deliver him and honor him.
With long life I will satisfy him,

And show him My salvation.
(Psalm 91:14-16)

Now listen how the Holy Spirit interpreted these scriptures to me. God is very personal.

Because Daffney has made Me her top priority above everyone and everything, I will not fail her. I will elevate my daughter to a spiritual level in Me beyond her comprehension. I will fill her with my anointing. Because I am familiar with her love for Me and my people. I enjoy our encounters. My daughter delights to spend quality time with her Papa. This always pleases Me. She and I have such a wonderful intimate relationship. Daffney has access to some of the deepest parts of Me. I have revealed who I AM to her.

Yes, I will answer my princess whenever she calls for me. Day or night, it doesn't matter what kind of troubles my child faces; I am going to bring her through every one of them. I will never break any of my oaths to her; this is my solemn promise to her. Together, we will successfully walk through her adversities. My handmaiden knows that I got her back. Afterward, I will give my baby girl unimaginable rewards and possibilities. She has accepted my Son as her personal Savior and Lord. Therefore, her life is endless, and she is all mine. I rejoice as I reward her with insuperable strength.

God so Loved the World

There is good news. The Father has extended an open invitation to humanity. God wants an intimate relationship with us. How cool is that? He desires to draw us closer unto Himself. The kindest Spirit on earth wants you. God wants everyone to experience His righteousness, calmness, peacefulness, sweetness, boldness, and connectedness.

Because of the sinful disobedience of Adam and Eve, there was a spiritual chasm between God and the children of men and women. *(Genesis Chapter 4)* Nevertheless, the Heavenly Father brilliantly created a wonderful and extraordinary plan of redemption to rescue and restore us. *For God so loved the world that he gave his one and only Son, that whoever believes in him shall not perish but have eternal life. (John 3:16)*

The Lord Jesus Christ descended from Heaven and came to the earth in the likeness of human flesh. He died on the cross for the sins of the world. Once and for all, Christ Jesus paid a hefty price to pardon the sin of humanity. The prophet Isaiah prophetically stated, *"Surely He has borne our griefs and carried our sorrows; Yet we esteemed Him stricken, Smitten by God, and afflicted. But He was wounded for our transgressions, He was bruised for our iniquities; The chastisement for our peace was upon Him, And by His stripes we are healed." (Isaiah 53:4-5)*

By the Holy Spirit of God, Christ Jesus was resurrected from the grave on the third day. He arose from the dead with all power and authority in His hand. What was stolen from Adam (power and authority within the earth realm) was recovered and restored by the Son of God. He is our atonement. Christ Jesus provided a way for everyone to come back into the original and harmonious relationship with the Ancient of Days. The victorious and finished work of Christ Jesus at the cross gave us a legal access of reconciliation with God the Father. What a wonderful gift to have full entrance to the true and living God who loves us dearly. *Jesus said to him, I am the way, the truth, and the life. No one comes to the Father except through Me. (John 14:6)*

Anyone who has accepted Christ Jesus is sealed by the Holy Spirit of God and is given everlasting life. The Holy Bible states that he or she is a new creation in Christ Jesus. Every sin has been nullified and wiped away by the blood of Christ Jesus. It is written, *without the shedding of His blood, there can be no remission of sins.*

(Hebrews 9:22) Eternal life in Christ Jesus is the believer's spiritual inheritance. *(Romans 6:22-23) (John 10:28)*

Since we are now joined to Christ, we have been given the treasures of redemption by his blood—the total cancellation of our sins—all because of the cascading riches of his grace. This superabundant grace is already powerfully working in us, releasing within us all forms of wisdom and practical understanding.

And through the revelation of the Anointed One, he unveiled his secret desires to us—the hidden mystery of his long-range plan, which he was delighted to implement from the very beginning of time. And because of God's unfailing purpose, this detailed plan will reign supreme through every period of time until the fulfillment of all the ages finally reaches its climax—when God makes all things new in all of heaven and earth through Jesus Christ.

Through our union with Christ we too have been claimed by God as his own inheritance. Before we were even born, he gave us our destiny; that we would fulfill the plan of God who always accomplishes every purpose and plan in his heart. God's purpose was that we Jews, who were the first to long for the messianic hope, would be the first to believe in the Anointed One and bring great praise and glory to God!

And because of him, when you who are not Jews heard the revelation of truth, you believed in the wonderful news of salvation. Now we have been stamped with the seal of the promised Holy Spirit. He is given to us like an engagement ring is given to a bride, as the first installment of what's coming! He is our hope-promise of a future inheritance which seals us until we have all of redemption's promises and experience complete freedom—all for the supreme glory and honor of God! (Ephesians 1:7-14)

Salvation through Repentance

If you desire to accept Christ Jesus as your Lord and Savior, please reiterate these words "I repent of all of my sins. I confess that I am a sinner, and I am in need of a loving Savior. By faith, I surrender my life to God. I confess with my mouth the Lord Jesus Christ, and believe in my heart that God has raised His beloved son Christ Jesus from the dead. I accept Him as my Lord and Savior." If you said the above-mentioned words and truly meant them from your heart, you are a born-again believer in Christ Jesus. It is that simple. You are saved by grace (unmerited favor) through faith (belief and trust in God). Salvation is a beautiful and eternal gift from God. *(Ephesians 2:8)*

Welcome to the Family of God!

Give thanks unto the Father, who has qualified us to be partakers of the inheritance of the saints in light: Who hath delivered us from the power of darkness, and hath translated us into the kingdom of his dear Son: In whom we have redemption through his blood, even the forgiveness of sins:

Who is the image of the invisible God, the firstborn of every creature: For by him were all things created, that are in heaven, and that are in earth, visible and invisible, whether they be thrones, or dominions, or principalities, or powers: all things were created by him, and for him: And he is before all things, and by him all things consist. And he is the head of the body, the church: who is the beginning, the firstborn from the dead; that in all things he might have the preeminence.

For it pleased the Father that in him should all fullness dwell; And, having made peace through the blood of his cross, by him to reconcile all things unto himself; by him, I say, whether they be things in earth, or things in heaven. And you, that were sometime alienated and enemies in your mind by wicked works, yet now hath he reconciled, in the body of his flesh through death, to present you holy and unblameable and unreproveable in his sight. (Colossians 1:12-22)

Now that you are a new believer in Christ Jesus. It is important for your spiritual growth to find a good bible teaching church. The church is a community of believers. They gather to fellowship and to learn the unadulterated good news of Christ Jesus. There is one triune God. He has three manifestations - God the Father, God the Son, and God the Holy Spirit dwelling in the believers. Each person of the Godhead walks in agreement, conjunction and coequality.

Baptism Water Immersion

Baptism is the next step after salvation through repentance. It is an outward sign of an inward change. It is compared to a burial. A symbol of a person dying from his or her past and beginning a new one as a Christian dedicated to God. Baptism Immersion in water, at most churches, is a public confession of your faith and a commitment to Christ Jesus. It expresses to the world that you love, trust, and hope in Him. It is a celebratory experience. *And this water symbolizes baptism that now saves you also—not the removal of dirt from the body but the pledge of a clear conscience toward God. It saves you by the resurrection of Jesus Christ. (1 Peter 3:21)* More scriptures pertaining to salvation to repentance and baptism are listed in the scripture reference section. A local Pastor or Church leader can provide you with additional information pertaining to baptism.

The Expectations of Prayer

Prayer is significant and a powerful tool of communicating with God. It's an on-going conversation between God and you. He talks, and you listen. Then you talk, and He listens. (I declare there are times when God allows me to know when He laughs). Sweet meditation of prayer, the Father will sing to you or give you words to a new song to sing to Him. As believers, we long to hear the sweetness of His still voice. Prayer aligns us to hear the voice of the Father. Equally important, God rejoices to hear our assorted voices. Our Heavenly Papa wants us to come to Him without trepidations. Prayer is the key and faith unlocks the Everlasting Door. His Holy Spirit and our spirts joined together in unity.

Through prayer, we confess sins, receive divine insightful revelations, touch in agreement for healings and deliverance, combine with fasting, yield to discipline, replenish strength, assist in spiritual warfare, praise and worship, sharpen discernment, increase energy, prevent distractions, produce peace, immobilize discouragement, eliminate worry and anxiety, provide directions, produce confidence, and so much more. Its abundant resources are infinite. Daily prayer allows us to share every aspect of our lives with the Father.

One might say why does God want us to pray to Him? He already knows everything. Yes, He does. Daily prayer is an act of worship and obedience. The Holy Bible tells the beloved of God to always rejoice, pray without ceasing and give thanks *in* (not for) all circumstances, for this is the will of God in Christ Jesus for you. (*1 Thessalonians 5:16-18)* When you pray by faith, you are participating in a genuine request made by God Himself. It makes Him happy. For all that He has done and will do for us, it's a blessing and privilege to reciprocate our gratitude toward Him.

New Heart from the Father

I will give you a new heart and put a new spirit within you; and I will remove the heart of stone from your flesh and give you a heart of flesh. (Ezekiel 36:26) We who are regenerated in Christ Jesus have been completely made over by the Holy Spirit of God. The new heart of flesh causes us to be sensitive and responsive to the Father's touch. If He makes a request, we accept and honor it.

The spirit-filled believer's new heart does not cease from praying, and it does not function in a ritualistic manner. The new heart is in alignment with the rhythm of God's heartbeat. Prayer becomes a lifestyle not an obligation. It is the very thing that brings us into the Presence of a Holy and Righteous God.

Father, I am grateful to know that you are with us. You are a God who sits high but looks low. You are concerned about everything that pertains to us. Thank you for blessing us with the Holy Spirit. It is a privilege to be cognizant of your Holy Presence. You are the water which continues to quench our thirst. Your majestic miracles are great. God, we adore you. And it is so, in Christ Jesus' name – Amen.

CHAPTER NINE
NOW, IT'S TIME
TO SOAR!

He says, "Be still and know that I am God;
I will be exalted among the nations, I will be exalted in the earth!"
(Psalm 46:10)

Early one Saturday morning, I went to Starbucks, because I had a taste for a peppermint latte with soy milk. This is one of my favorite drinks. As I approached the cashier ready to place an order, I hesitated. I thought I had cut in front of a lady. Quickly, I apologized to her. I discovered that she came into the coffee shop after I did; she was to be served next.

I ordered and paid for my drink. Then, I stepped to the side to wait for it to be made. The same lady came over and started a conversation. We introduced ourselves to each other. Her name was LeAnn. We discussed my up and coming women's conference. I invited her to the conference and gave her a copy of the flyer. She was very interested and asked some questions about it. LeAnn was very pleasant to talk to. She gave good eye contact. Her energy was positive and warm. I didn't want our conversation to end. It was one of those special moments.

LeAnn wanted to know the denomination of my church. I answered, "Assemblies Church of God." She happily stated, "I am a Catholic." She was filled with excitement. LeAnn had just left early morning service. Her smile was contagious. During our conversation, I thought what a lovely woman. We had good chemistry.

The different denominations meant nothing to us. God was the center of our focus. We blessed His name. We praised, smiled and laughed about His goodness. When LeAnn lifted one of her hands up, I saw that she was missing some fingers. I was caught off guard and saddened by the deformity of her hand. Quickly, I looked back into her beautiful eyes to distract my curiosity. I didn't want to be flippant. However, I knew I had to look at it again.

As LeAnn lifted her hand again, I mustered up enough courage to ask what happened to it. I learned that she had a blood disorder. It was life threatening, very painful, and at times unbearable. She prayed and cried many days and nights for God to heal her. Regardless of her prognosis, she wanted to live and not die. She needed a miracle.

This is exactly what God gave her. He spared her life. LeAnn thanked God for providing her with additional time on earth to spend with her loving husband and warmhearted children. She knew that it could have been the other way. LeAnn worked diligently to regain her independence. She is a walking miracle. Prayer by faith gave her the hope and fortitude to stand strong through one of the worst situations of her life.

Our conversation was priceless. We grabbed our drinks and walked slowly toward one of the entrance doors. We continued to praise God for His goodness. Afterward, we hugged and said our good-byes. LeAnn's testimony provides true meaning of adamant faith in Christ Jesus. Despite her tragedy, it has not stopped her from praising Him. That morning at Starbucks, she sprinkled doses of heavenly sunshine into my life. In life, we get to experience some pertinent moments. There are some decent people who cross our paths for short moments of time. These occurrences are to be cherished.

Our testimonies are great tools to share with others. They allow us to brag about the sovereignty of God. At my first speaking engagement as a minister, I decided to share a portion of my personal testimony. I was a bit nervous, because, I had not shared it publicly before. After the microphone was handed to me, the fear left. As I began to share my testimony, I disclosed some of the most painful parts of it. The congregations' eyes were fastened upon me. They listened to my every word. The church was very quiet. If someone dropped a pin, you would have heard it. Eventually, one of my relatives broke the silence by making sobbing sounds. She was surprised and had no idea that I suffered to that extent.

Days later, my mother received a telephone call from one of the church members. She described how others shared their personal and painful testimonies. The lady rejoiced and stated how they were released from their bondage. She was thankful that I boldly shared my story, for it had a powerful effect on their lives. Our testimonies are to be used as sling shots and rocks against the attacks of the adversary. They display the continuing greatness of God.

Faith to Soar

An eagle is a large bird with powerful wings. Impressively, its range of speed is between 35-43mph. When it hunts for prey, it can dive into the water at a speed of 75-99 mph. The neat thing about an eagle is its keen sense of knowledge. Way in advance, it knows when a storm is approaching before it materializes. It searches for and flies to a very high spot.

The eagle's eyes continue to look upward waiting for the winds to come. As soon as they appear, the eagle releases its wings to allow the winds to pick them up. Then, the winds lift it above the storm. While the storm rages beneath it, the eagle soars above the storm. Soaring allows us to take leaps of faith. Soaring allows us to believe God even when you can't trace Him. Soaring allows us to dream for big things. Soaring allows us to embrace every waking moment of our lives. Soaring allows us to release the past and embrace the present. Soaring allows us to rest and reflect.

Faith and Its effect

I have repetitiously utilized the word "faith." Faith is complete trust and confidence in God. One of the biblical scriptures which defines faith states that it is the substance of things hoped for, the evidence of things not seen. *(Hebrews 11:1)* Here's how God simplified faith and its effect to me. "Faith is the impossible made possible. The unseen into the seen." Faith has nothing to do with our sensuality. It is not based on our emotions and feelings. It can't be bought, sold, or purchased. The more you read His Word; the more you will hear His voice. The more you hear His voice; the more you will believe in Him. The more you believe in Him; the more your faith will grow. The more your faith grows; the more you will reach higher heights in God. *(Romans 10:17)* Faith brings you closer to God's heart. Without it, we can't please our Heavenly Father. *(Hebrews 11:6)*

Does a believer's faith in God always remain at the same level? No. Sometimes, our faith will fluctuate. The Lord said, "His grace is enough." Whenever, we are weak He is strong. *(2 Corinthians 12:9)* During difficult times, you might want to succumb to anything that brings comfort. Because, the trial seems unbearable. It might appear like you won't make it through them. Especially when the situations have existed for a longer period of time. This is when the spirit of doubt deceitfully rears its ugly head. It speaks against God in a demeaning and cunning way. The main goal of doubt is to fill your heart and mind with uncertainties about God. It whispers into your ear that the faith thing might work for some people, but it will never work for you. Don't believe its deceptions, for this stronghold is a lying weasel. God said that He will not keep any good thing from those who love Him. *(Psalm 84:11)* Hold on! Help is coming.

Difficult trials will cause the average person to scream and holler. This stage is called "faith being tried and tested by the fire." I am quite sure many of you have heard this adage, "if it's not one thing, it's another." During this period of time, the only word that might be mustered up is Jesus or help. Other times, there are no words but a deep sigh or a groan. God vowed that the fire (struggle), will not burn (destroy) us. He didn't say that we would not feel the intensity of its heat.

Many people that I know, explained what it felt like being in the midst of insurmountable hardships. They used these three words: helpless, hopeless, and fearful. At times, they felt all alone. Some of them wanted to die. The one thing they had was faith in God. It carried them through the tough days. Without it, they could not have made it. Faith is like a bright light in the darkest of time. It gives us the awareness that Abba Father is closer than we think.

Faith doesn't exempt us from trials, but it helps us to go through them. Our trials can be used for spiritual growth. We learn from the Holy Spirit how to pray, believe, hope, trust, wait, and depend on the Lord even the more. When we properly go through them with our eyes on Christ Jesus, they produce godly characteristics, resilience, strength, wisdom, knowledge, understanding, discretion, tenacity, and the list goes on. These attributes are priceless and endless jewels within us for eternity.

The wisdom of faith teaches that tribulations will not destroy us. It will eliminate anything that is not needed for our next level. Faith in the Lord gently reminds us to never make any problems bigger than the Sovereign God. Faith in Him helps us to soar.

God's Chosen Generation

It was recorded in the Holy Bible that God wanted a special group of people who would willingly serve Him. He would be their God, and they would be His very own people. Each of them would have the opportunity to experience an intimate and everlasting relationship with their Heavenly Father. His people were expected to learn and live by His principles, laws, statutes, and commands. God promised to compensate them with a fruitful land, protection, health, prosperity, and good success. As His representatives, they would exemplify, to other pagan nations, the true meaning of righteous living. God selected a gentleman by the name of Abram to assist with His plan. The man and his wife, Sari, would bring forth the chosen seed, and his name shall be called "Isaac." In Hebrew, his name means "Laughter." The Great I AM promised Abram that his descendants would be more than the number of the stars in the sky and the grains of sand by the seashore. Here's the dilemma, Abram and Sari were old and barren. They desperately wanted to have a child. At that stage in their lives, they had given up on their dream. Nevertheless, they accepted and believed the ridiculous plan of God.

As the biblical story advances, we learn that Sari got tired of waiting on God - I am not throwing shade, but this is exactly how we feel at times. Let's get back to the story. She thought God was taking too long. Days, weeks, months and years, she waited and hoped for His promise. Nothing materialized but discomfort and agony. Eventually, she became frustrated. The one thing that she wanted to give to her husband seemed unattainable. In biblical times, a woman was measured by the number of children she birthed.

Out of desperation, she formulated a strategy to attempt to solve her fertility deficiency. She asked her husband to impregnate her servant Hagar. Abram was given permission by his wife to have a sexual encounter with another woman. Together Abram and Hagar would produce a child. Her husband agreed. I know what some of you ladies are thinking, but in those days, this kind of child bearing behavior was culturally accepted. The child would legally belong to Abram and Sari. However, this was not the will of God for their lives. Their child would come by supernatural means.

Hagar, got pregnant and had a son. They named him Ishmael. In Hebrew, his name means "God listens." You can imagine how elated Abram was. At last, he had a child. Abram, Hagar and Ishmael spent a lot of family time together, but Sari was still at the core of his affections. Eventually, the servant woman became jealous and rebelled against her boss lady. Miss Thing thought she had leverage because of her new position as the biological mother of Abram's only son. Abram's household was faced with baby mama drama.

Nevertheless, the spoken word of God came to fruition. Sari and Abram became pregnant at the age of 90 and 100 years old. As a sign of His promise to them, the Heavenly Father changed Abram's name to Abraham (father of many nations) and Sari's name to Sarah (mother of nations). Because of strong opposition in their household, Hagar and Ishmael were forced to leave. This saddened Abraham. God vowed to watch over Ishmael, and His sacred promise comforted Abraham. He knew that God would always be faithful to His oath. (*Genesis chapters 12-18, 21 and Deuteronomy 7:1-9*)

Whatever God promises, you can trust in Him. Even if your storm displays the opposite, you can always use your spiritual weapons by faith. Believe, speak, and resist the trappings of frustration and desperation. They are subtle plots to keep you from soaring. Their ultimate purpose is to impede the way you view the inerrant words of God. Within their perimeters, it is hard to think in a rational way. This is what Sari experienced. Frustration redirected her thoughts against His desired plan. Desperation showed her a mental picture of God not being able to keep His promise.

These two adversarial strongholds from the enemy, work diligently to trump the faith of believers. To keep their eyes affixed on personal problems and not on God's agenda. However, we are not ignorant to the devices of the adversary. (*2 Corinthians 2:11*) Our Papa tells us to submit to Him, resist the devil, and that joker must flee. (*James 4:7*) Remain focused and soar high!

King David's testimony about the deliverance power of God against frustration and desperation.

If the LORD had not been on our side, let Israel say if the LORD had not been on our side when people attacked us, they would have swallowed us alive when their anger flared against us; the flood would have engulfed us, the torrent would have swept over us, the raging waters would have swept us away. Praise be to the LORD, who has not let us be torn by their teeth. We have escaped like a bird from the fowler's snare; the snare has been broken, and we have escaped. Our help is in the name of the LORD, the Maker of heaven and earth. (Psalm 124)

If you have been given a divine word from God, it must come to pass! Stand on your Father's timeless and treasured promises. God will never fail you, for He is faithful. His words reign forever. He will never deviate from them. His word is His bond.

A Rhema Word from God

"The Lord God is speaking to you right now. Trust and believe in Me. I know what I am doing. I have been working situations out from generation to generation. Keep your eyes on me! Faithfulness is not what I do. It is who I am. Your situations are never too hard for Me to handle. As I worked things out for Abraham and Sarah, I vow to work them out for you too. Be consistent, for I AM! says the Lord."

Significant Information

There is a vital lesson we can learn from the story of Abraham and Sarah. Be careful not to make a permanent decision in a temporary situation. It is a recipe for failure.

Stress, Fear and Depression

One of my college professors gave my classmates and me an assignment about stress. She wanted us to explain in our own words how we handle stress. Below is a small portion of what I wrote.

"I have faced many insurmountable situations in my life. For years, I attempted to work them out from an emotional point of view. Instead of my circumstances changing for the better, they plummeted into a downward spiral. I wasted a lot of precious time worrying about things which had not materialized. The result of it opened the door to stress, fear, and depression.

The overwhelming torments from them brought abnormal thoughts. They robbed me of a sound mind. I gave away golden opportunities because they bound and placed me into a lonely pit for countless years. Stress became an uninvited visitor; it overstayed its welcome. Fear hovered over me constantly, and depression held me as its prisoner. Thank God, they no longer have any rights over me. I took back my authority and power from them.

How do I cope with the burden of stress? I trust and place my faith in God. In prayer, I give those heavy mindboggling issues to Him. Christ Jesus is my problem solver. He is a very present help in the time of trouble. This is the only reason why I can soar above the pressures of stress. I am mighty grateful to know that He cares so much about me."

I hoped the above writing assignment would not offend my professor, for she was an Orthodox Jewish woman. It did not bother her. She thought it was very insightful, and I received an "A." In addition, she was very curious about my faith in Christ Jesus. I love how God creates various ways for His children to share His unconditional love with others.

Call to Ministry

In June 2008 while cleaning my bedroom, I had a divine visitation from the Lord. I gingerly sat down on my bed, for I wanted to give Him my full attention. Internally, His still small voice said, "I have given you a ministry."

I was humbly touched. I said, "Lord I am nobody. There are others who are wiser than I am. Many of them are financially situated. I am a divorced woman twice and faced with different struggles." My disparaging labels meant nothing to Him. They were like sound bites.

He said, "I give you my Word. I AM with you. I will supply everything that you need. Step out by faith and trust in Me. You do not have to fear. Whoever blesses your ministry, I will bless them. Whoever attempts to curse it, I will curse them.

The ministry which I have given to you will be used as a catalyst unto good fruit. It will be a deliverance, healing, and restoration outreach. You will provide an atmosphere for my children to feel safe and to freely praise Me. Then, I will work supernatural miracles as they worship Me."

Without hesitation, I said, "yes Lord." I loved the Lord, and the opportunity to serve Him and His people was an honor and a pleasure. I was given permission to name it "Only the King Can Do It Ministry." Truly, He can do anything.

I shared the above-mentioned words with some of my friends and acquaintances. They listened and asked questions. They agreed to assist me. I will never forget when we had our first ministry meeting. Everyone was filled with anticipation and exhilaration about the conference preparation. Until **that** question was asked. What is our budget? I had a smirk grin on my face. Then, I lifted one hand up in the air and used two fingers to make a zero sign. They were a bit shocked. However, they agreed to continue to support my mission. Our meeting ended in hope, faith, and trust in God.

Days later, people started to generously donate to my ministry. Their acts of love and kindness touched our hearts. It was phenomenal. Because of my obedience unto the Lord, our first event was successful. The day of the event, I walked around the beautiful church in amazement. God had opened the window of Heaven; He blessed us with everything that was needed.

During the service, His people praised, clapped, sang, and smiled. They made a joyful noise unto their Savior. My heart was filled with gratitude; this was exactly what God wanted.

This is how I soar: When, people are snatched away from the devil and accept Christ Jesus as their personal Savior and Lord. When, people rededicate their lives to Him. When, people praise and worship Him. When, people are encouraged to hold on to His unchanging hands. When, people are delivered and set free from their painful past. When, people receive miraculous healings and other breakthroughs. When, people are filled with gratitude. When, I know that God is pleased, this especially does my heart good. How do you soar?

Prayer

Father, you are amazingly good. Thank you for showing us how to soar by faith. You have done wonderful and mighty things in the lives of your people. God, we are humbled by your glory. I ask you to permeate every inch of us with your joy, peace, and righteousness in the Holy Spirit. And it is so, in Christ Jesus' name – Amen.

CHAPTER TEN
LIVING YOUR BEST LIFE
AND ENJOYING YOURSELF

*I can do all things through Christ who strengthens me
(Philippians 4:13)*

Early one beautiful snowy morning, I got out of my warm and cozy bed. I must say that I was enthused and ready to share my heart with you. Each chapter of my book allowed me to revisit certain portions of my life. Some of them were a bit sad; other chapters made me smile while shaking my head. I found them to be somewhat amusing.

As I write to you this morning, I am grateful to be operating out of wholeness. My mind is fresh with positive thoughts and a healthier attitude. Life through my lens looks clearer and better. It doesn't mean that I don't have hiccups along the way. They are fewer in number and less in duration. There are three helpful techniques that continue to play a significant role in my life: meditation, gratitude, and evolution.

Insightful Tips for Successful Living

Meditation helps to alleviate distractions and anxieties. I love to meditate in my living room or bedroom. I retreat from the world around me. I make sure my phone is on vibrate or completely turned off. The television and social media are disengaged. My total attention is directed towards God.

The quietness in the room causes my thoughts to be stilled. Eventually, my mind becomes restful and peaceful. My eyes are closed. My soul waits on God to quicken my spirit and draw me closer to Him. As I am elevated, His presence saturates my entire being. I sense and know that He is in the room, for there is such a peacefulness.

I become hungry and thirsty. It is almost like I am starving for Him. I listen to His voice which sounds like a soft whisper. After His voice fades away, I repeat scriptures, weep with joy, praise His name, or sit in silence. There is such a positive energy in the room.

There is an overwhelming sense of calmness within my soul. This is when it feels like I am weightlessly floating in the air. After meditation, I am energetic and full of confidence to face my day or night. Nothing in this world compares to it effects.

Gratitude is regarded as one of the highest inner contentment principles. Appreciation fills your life with everything good. Gratitude vitalizes the spirit and soul. It releases dopamine into the brain and body. Gratefulness enhances psychological health. It brings forth happiness and strengthens our emotions. In addition, it increases self-esteem and works against self-centeredness. Gratitude makes people friendlier and eliminates jealous and envious feelings.

Thankfulness provides us with an unstoppable edge. It helps us to relax and improves sleep. It refines our decision-making and causes us to strive for excellence. Gratitude unlocks the beauty of life.

Evolution is a part of life. Advancement welcomes the door to new opportunities of growth and developments. It helps you not to be afraid to take risks by hopping, skipping, and jumping into your future with optimism. Evolution motivates us to learn and gain knowledge about the world that we live in. It influences us to travel to different places near and far. Expansion dares us to go outside of our places of familiarity.

Evolution teaches how not to stare at the cracked mirror of impossibilities. It helps us to avoid traps of stagnation by quickly identifying and eliminating them. If you fail to reach a desired goal, determination makes you shake the dust off your feet and try again.

Living and Enjoying your Life with Others

Family is very significant. They are an asset. Each family member should be loved and accepted. Moreover, they are to be regarded with the highest of respect. In times of disagreement, each party should listen carefully and not try to think of answers for retaliation purposes. They should be careful of hurtful words that proceed from their mouths. Negative words can be painful and detrimental. The bond which holds the unit together should not be severed by frivolous drama. The kinship is very special. Friends can be selected, but family members are an extension of where you came from.

No family member should be intimidated or feel not valued. The relationship should be knitted and stitched firmly in love. Protection and safety should be readily available. Family members should display unity through the toughest of time. In addition, it is important not to call a loved one only during rough times. Family is one of the most important relationships upon this earth. Much work is needed to keep them as the top priority. For they are priceless and greatly needed for the overall stability of the world.

Now, all of us have some relatives who are toxic. You have cried, carried, waited, and attempted to address their unhealthy issues. They refuse to listen to you. They have drained you spiritually, emotionally, psychologically, physiologically, relationally, and financially. These family members need to be loved from a distance. Give them over to the Lord in prayer. If your toxic loved one is someone very close to you or lives in your household, keep him or her in your prayers - Do not pray anxiously and forcefully for them - but let God be God. He will not fail you! Your job is to protect your mind and heart - nothing should disrupt your peace.

Good friendships are the best. They might not have a biological connection to you, but sometimes, some of your friends can be closer than family members. They are vital to your life. Through thick or thin, they got your back. They love you for who you are. When you are around them, you can be your authentic self. They aren't jealous by your gifts and talents, nor are they ashamed of your shortcomings.

During disagreements or confrontations, they get frustrated and disappointed with you or vice a versa. Alone time is needed to ponder and reflect about the different sides of view. True friends will eagerly accept apologies and politely delineate their own faults. Against all odds, they will continue to cheer you on. These folks are to be treasured and never taken for granted. They want you to succeed in life and willingly volunteer their time, finances, or effort to help you succeed.

Decent associates are needed in our lives. They are not your closest friends, but they are good-hearted folks. Associates do not necessarily have to absorb a lot of your time and energy. They are easy to talk to and live by a set standard of ethics. There is a mutual respect between you and them. Some of them are in our lives for a short or long season. There is a reason why we need to connect with them. Their wisdom might be the information needed to take you into your next level in life. I have learned a lot from them.

Don't forget to laugh. For God's sake, don't take yourself too seriously. Laughter allows us to smell the roses and enjoy their scents. Laughter is contagious. Some mornings before I go to work,

I get a chance to talk to my daughter-in-love Brenda. We laugh about the silliest of things. Before we end our conversation, I say, "have a delicious day and don't forget to smile." It doesn't matter what kind of mood she is in. Brenda smiles and lets out a sound of laughter followed by some giggles. The Holy Bible states that a *cheerful heart is life good medicine, but a broken spirit dries up the bones. (Proverbs 17:22)*

Have you ever laughed until the muscle in your belly ached? I mean that you couldn't stop laughing to get a word or two out of your mouth. Others around you smiled and laughed but didn't know why you were laughing. They were kept in suspense until you conveyed what tickled you. I love those moments!

Sometimes, I like to watch the Andy Griffith television show (to the younger readers, google it). My favorite character is Barney Fife. Deputy Fife is overanxious and hilarious. He does some of the silliest things with his facial expressions and body movements. He doesn't think pragmatically. However, he believes that he is very witty. Barney thinks everyone needs his assistance. I can't help laughing out loud at his mishaps. Afterward, my heart goes out to him when he feels rejected and disregarded. My children laugh at me for watching this show. Have you had your doses of laughter for today? See, I made you smile – allow laughter to continue to flow out of your belly and laugh out loud.

Habitation of Praise and Worship. It is vitally important for praise and worship to be at the center of our lives. They invite the presence of God. Daily, the two are a great force to be reckoned with. They bring us closer to the Darling of Heaven. They refocus our minds. Praise and worship strengthen our faith in Christ Jesus. Both can be utilized in the fiercest of battles. Even in sorrow, they release supernatural power and strength.

Praise allows us to give thanks and honor to Him. The Holy Bible demands every living creature to praise the LORD. We glorify God for His characteristics and mighty acts of kindness. We give Father God the respect that is owed to Him, and our praises help to make His name famous by promoting His love and goodness. *Worship* comes from a special place, deep within our spirits. It demands us to humble ourselves before the Almighty God. Quality time alone with Father Abba is a requirement. To be true worshippers of God, we must surrender every part of our lives to Him. The price is very costly, but the reward is marvelous.

A Story of Hope

There was a lady name Patricia who always felt like she did not measure up to others. She was very defensive. The truth is Patricia was difficult to love. At times, she was a bit abrasive with her own words. She always thought that she was right. She withdrew from her loved ones and friends. Patricia started to nitpick at other people's bloopers and inconsistencies. Somehow, she overlooked her own faults. She developed a callous heart. The girl was full of herself. Pride became the focus of her life. It was a coping mechanism which covered her deep-rooted pain.

One day she decided to get some professional help from a responsible person. This was the first time she felt safe and at ease. The reliable person did not degrade but accepted her. Patricia opened her heart and surrendered to her vulnerability. Through wise counseling, Patricia learned that life was not meant to be lived inside of a bubble. She needed to reach out to others and to avoid being the center of attention. She was not an uncaring person, but a wounded individual.

Patricia had to be responsible by letting go of her debilitating thoughts. It was necessary not to hide her faulty thoughts and feelings. How did she do it? Patricia prayed and worked closely with her counselor to change her distorted thought patterns. Studiously, she discovered what her triggers were. Patricia understood that she was a product of her environment. She grew-up in a household where each of her family members lived in strife, contention, distrust, and a lack of love. Both of her parents were alcoholics. They were distant and aloof toward each other and their five children. There were never hugs or affirmations. Her father had been adopted and sexually and mentally abused. He verbally abused Patricia and her siblings. She carried a lot of resentment against her parents. She released her heavy load and forgave her parents. Now, she thrives from a healthier place. She has a determined will to remain on the pathway of wholeness. Patricia and her husband have a loving relationship. She is the proud mother of a son and daughter. God can heal anyone.

The Rewards of Forgiveness

I have experienced betrayal. God knows nothing can cut like it. To trust someone who viciously, willfully, and wreckfully afflicts agony upon you, goes beyond anything imaginable. These folks knew my weaknesses and purposefully used them against me. It was painful and wicked.

My mind was tormented by their hurtful acts. For years, I relived each of the awful occurrences as if they just happened. I had many sleepless nights which were filled with tears and mental discomfort. I thought I was never going to get well. I smiled when I wanted to cry, and I hid my true feelings and emotions within me. I was in agony. I walked around life with a wounded heart, for I gave those haters too much of my attention. I overly and excessively talked about them.

I wanted to be delivered from the stronghold of unforgiveness. It was serious. It placed a wedge between God and me. To receive healing, I had to forgive my offenders. God will never tell His children to do something without supplying the strength and power to perform it. He knew some offenses would be difficult to forgive based on our own personal strength. Thank God for the Holy Spirit who assisted me. Through His strength, I took the power away from my attackers by choosing to forgive them. I didn't condone their acts. I gave them to Christ Jesus to judge as He decided.

Through consistent prayer and determination, their malicious attacks were wiped away from my memory. I was able to go days without thinking about them. Whether in a crowd of people or alone, I had full control of my thoughts. The rest is history. I only revisited my offenders' negative offenses if I needed to share those hurtful experiences with others. I knew I was free from them, because I didn't have ambiguous feelings.

Also, I suffered with unforgiveness towards myself. I was in a lot of financial debt. I made a lot of unhealthy decisions. This caused me to be submerged under a pile of debt. It affected my life in every aspect. I could not see my way through it. Then, I prayed and asked the Lord to assist me. I confessed my wrong doings, and I asked the Father to show me where I had failed. I asked Him to teach me how to be a better steward over my finances. Then, I devised a plan to get out of debt. I worked hard to bring it to fruition. I must confess some of my debts were washed away by the favor of God's grace. I stayed on a plan to pay off the other ones. They disappeared little by little. I must say freedom from debt feels good.

When I was in debt, I spoke as if the bills were already paid. I am a woman who lives by faith. I want to remind folks who are currently struggling in debt that His grace and mercy will work in this area too. Even if you made a financial mistake, please know that you are covered by the blood of Christ Jesus. Seek guidance from God; come up with a pragmatic plan; find a financial consultant or read financial books. For God's sake, don't allow the enemy of your soul to tell you that your case is hopeless. The devil is a liar. Focusing too much attention on the enemy makes the possibility of debt cancellation appear impossible. There is nothing impossible for God.

Spoken Words by Faith

While going through the healing process of forgiveness and debt cancellation, I spoke selective words by faith. I said them silently and verbally. They became etched into my spirit.

"I refuse to be the prisoner of unforgiveness. I speak against any false attacks which attempt to hold me captive. I walk in the authority and power of the Holy Spirit. I have unlimited strength to forgive my offenders. Therefore, I exercise the right to release them. I am free from every one of their offenses. I no longer occupy invisible pitfalls of shame and guilt. My chains have been broken, and my shackles have been removed. My soul is at rest and my mind is clear. My thoughts are regulated by the Spirit of truth. He helps me to honor the law of forgiveness. Unforgiveness is a defeated foe. I will not look backward but forward. I have excelled in every area of my life.

I have forgiven myself for getting into debt. I have already forgiven those who deceitfully led me into the snares of debt. I refuse to listen to the enemy of my soul concerning my financial status. Every debt has been resolved. In my house, every bill is paid on time. I have a healthier bank account. I am the lender and not the borrower. I have a surplus of money. I will generously donate to others. I live a life of productivity. Good success, prosperity, and the favor of God surrounds me like a blanket. I am equipped by Heaven's Best."

Living your best life and enjoying yourself means to focus on the simple and the intangible things of life. They are things which exist outside of the natural realm. Yet when applied into our daily lives, they make life much more meaningful and interesting.

Father, your love and kindness go beyond our comprehension. It guides us into the deepest and safest places within You. God, in your hand is the blue print for successful living. Those who are at crossroads, provide them with wisdom, knowledge, and understanding. Let your true light be their guide. And it is so, in Christ Jesus' name – Amen.

CHAPTER ELEVEN
FORGETTING YOUR PAST
AND MOVING FORWARD

*Forgetting those things which are behind you
and reaching for those things which are ahead.
(Philippians 3:13)*

While I was married to Tim many years ago, I suffered from a nervous breakdown. It had complete reign over me. My brain and mind went into an overkill of relentless thinking. My own thoughts collectively fought against me. There was nothing that I could do to regulate them. The enemy of my soul fought against me with extreme vengeance, deceptions, and accusations. This is what he does. He waits and searches for opportunities to strike against us at our weakest moments. The plot of his scheme was to get me to not believe and reject Christ Jesus as the Son of God. If I complied, he offered me a life of wealth and prosperity.

Prior to my nervous breakdown episode, I was abruptly awakened late one night. I attempted to go back to sleep, but I could not. I laid in my bed restless and quiet. Tim laid next to me sound asleep. After a while, I decided to get out of my bed to go downstairs. As I walked down the upstairs hallway, my attention was diverted to the direction of my children's bedrooms. I wanted to make sure they were okay. Toney, Travis, and Teron were asleep and snuggled under their covers.

I walked slowly down the stairs through the kitchen into the dining room area. I turned on the light switch, grabbed the Holy Bible and placed it on top of our dining room table. I sat down and enjoyed the concise "me time", for my children were young and demanded a lot of my attention. There was such a peacefulness that saturated the room. It filled my heart.

I read some scriptures, closed the Holy Bible, and prayed. During prayer, I was warned by the Spirit of God that I was going to be tested by a trial and placed into a prison for ten days. It was going to be a difficult experience. A nominal group of people would be given permission to visit me. My children would be safe and taken care of. The Lord promised that I was going to successfully walk through it unharmed. After this divine message, I knew whatever I had to endure was inevitable. I will never forget what happened next.

The room was filled with an eerie aura of darkness. I was very frightened. The fear continued to escalate. Then, my body shook and shivered uncontrollably. When I opened my mouth, my teeth chattered. I attempted to stop my legs from shaking by placing my hands on them. I was not able to stop my body movements. I was paralyzed by a stronghold of fear. Internally, I heard a broken sound. It was my voice. I cried out to Christ Jesus for His help. I said, "Jesus help me, rescue me....Lord, help....Help me....Oh God.... What is happening to me? Father, I need your help."

As I continued to cry inwardly to Him, my body was relieved and returned to its original state. God is my witness, I gained control over my body. Fear was eliminated, and calmness and peace reoccurred in the room. I praised and thanked God quietly. After that, I sat in the room for a few minutes. I tried to make sense of what had occurred. Unable to comprehend it, I decided to get back into my bed and go to sleep.

Everything seemed normal as I climbed the stairs and went back into my bedroom. As I laid in my bed, I still could not go back to sleep. Little did I know that the something else unexplainable had begun. For ten days, I encountered a disorder of rotating thoughts. For 24 hours per day, the thoughts continued to flood my mind. My days were filled with restlessness, and the nights I suffered from sleep deprivation. Have you ever wanted to go to sleep, but you could not? If yes, you can understand how miserable I was. In addition to the above-mentioned circumstance, I didn't have a good appetite. The stress was harsh on my body. Day by day I became weaker.

My parents were greatly concerned (especially my mother) about me. Mama said that she didn't want me to suffer. She was determined to be there for me. I was grateful for her help. (By this time, my parents were believers in Christ Jesus) She and daddy prayed vehemently for me. My mother reached out to another sister in Christ. She too called on the name of Jesus and prayed for me.

Late one night while lying down on my bed, a creepy thought entered my mind and frightened me. I was exasperated by it. I got out of my bed, walked to the door, and turned the door knob. I had no idea that my parents were outside of my bedroom door. As soon as I opened the door, my mother's hand was reaching towards the door knob. When I saw them, I was afraid and cried like a baby. God knows I was elated to see my parents.

I wanted to share with them what had occurred. My mother did not allow me to talk. She insisted that I open my mouth. She placed a couple of pills into my mouth and asked me to drink some water. I obeyed. Once again, I attempted to explain what antagonized me. My parents encouraged me to get some rest and made sure I laid down. I didn't go to sleep, but I felt a bit safer knowing that they were there. All I wanted was to be healed and to raise my children.

Later, I learned that my mother gave me some pills which were supposed to calm my nerves down. One thing for sure, those pills did nothing for me. My body rejected them, and the thoughts continued to control my mind. One evening, Tim and I were sitting in the dining room having a conversation. I recalled that I was weak but very chatty. He knew that my condition was serious by some of the questions that I had asked. For the first time in our marriage, he cried in front of me. Tim didn't know how to assist me. He called and spoke to one of his relatives who worked in the medical field. He was informed to seek professional help for me. It would have to be my choice to agree to it.

One afternoon my mother came over to do my laundry and other household chores. From my bedroom, I heard her as she walked back and forth calling on the "real Jesus." Each time, I heard "the real Jesus" I cried and shook my head in agreement. I couldn't verbalize how much I needed and wanted Him to rescue me. I was lost in the burden of my plight; it was traumatic. However, His name gave me some relief. The name of Jesus floated from the downstairs to the upstairs of my house. I had enough strength to get out of my bed. I stumbled and held on to furniture and the walls as I headed into the direction of my bedroom door.

I walked slowly and sluggishly down the upstairs hallway that led to the stairway. Each step I held tightly to the stairway handle to support my weight. My mother heard my footsteps. She didn't walk over to assist or express how happy she was to see me. She kept calling on His name. She knew it stimulated me. When I walked into the living room, our eyes locked. She asked me to sit down and help fold some washcloths. My mother thought it would keep my mind focused. When Tim and my Dad arrived and came back into the house, they were surprised, but happy to see me up and working. I was not totally out of the battle yet.

My father took a leave of absence from work to assist me. I loved the connection between him and my children. God knows my father loved his grandchildren. There were a lot of smiles and laughter when granddaddy came to visit them. Daddy was a big help during the daytime. Overall, his job was to supervise me. To make sure I was okay.

Although I was weak and filled with irritable thoughts, I had enough vigor to get Toney and Travis ready for school. I did okay -- except for the time when I forgot to put on one of Toney's socks. Daddy and Teron did things around the house as I attempted to rest. I can't really remember the amount of house cleaning my father did, if any at all. It was a blessing to have him during my time of need.

One day, my father encouraged me to lay down and try to get some rest. I selected to lay down in my oldest son Toney's bedroom. It was a bit dark because the mini blinds were closed. As I lay staring off into the abyss, a bible scripture arose in my mind. *For God has not given us a spirit of fear, but of power and of love and of a sound mind. (2 Timothy 1:7)* Hallelujah! Hallelujah, for the first time, a scripture entered my mind. I started inwardly praying and crying out to the Father. God, I want a sound mind. God, I need a sound mind. Father God, please give me a sound mind. I need your help. I am in trouble. Help me. Then, I said, "God heal me. I need you to heal my mind. I believe you can heal me. I don't doubt your powers. I know you can do it."

My father came into the bedroom to check on me. As he tiptoed into the room, he noticed that my eyes were open. He greeted me with a smile and sat on the edge of Toney's bed. He proceeded to tell me how he came into the bedroom twice. He noticed that I was asleep. My father said that I had slept for a couple of hours. This was strange, for I knew that I didn't fall asleep. He said, "Twinkles,

I came into the room and stood over you twice. You were sound asleep." This made daddy happy, for he knew that I was deprived of sleep.

Our conversation ended and silence filled the bedroom. My father got up from the edge of the bed, walked over to Toney's bedroom window and opened the mini blinds. He said, "let some of this Heavenly sunshine enter in this room." Then, daddy walked out of the bedroom. I will never forget what occurred next.

My son's dark bedroom was replaced by the brightness of the sunlight. The light was breathtaking! I sat up in his bed to enjoy the abundancy of the light. I stared at it as if I hadn't seen it in a while. I was amazed at how fast the darkness in the room faded away. Effortlessly, I got out of the bed to walk over to the window. There was a big tree in our front yard. I looked at it for a while. Then, I noticed how green the grass was. I looked up at the clear blue sky. The birds chirped. The flowers were beautiful. It was a gorgeous summer day. It felt like everything was brand new.

I realized that something different had occurred deep within me. I had energy, and my mind was at peace. Those horrible uncontrollable thoughts were gone. I knew that I was healed and delivered. I knew that God had rescued me. I knew that I was going to make it. I would be able to raise my own children with clarity of mind.

When my dad returned to the room, I was glad to see him. I let him know how I felt. He witnessed that I had a burst of energy, and I was able to hold a sensible conversation with him. I was not fearful but hopeful. He smiled and rejoiced. Daddy agreed that everything was going to be okay. We knew that a miracle had taken place. There is nothing like having a clear and peaceful mind. Nothing like it. After ten days, I was delivered from the uncontrollable thoughts and sleep deprivation. God is faithful to His word. Trust in Him!

After my major breakthrough, I agreed to meet with a psychiatrist. Weeks later, my daddy generously drove my children and me to my doctor's appointment. He offered to watch my munchkins during my counseling session. When I arrived at the doctor's office, Tim was already there. As usual, he was dressed professionally. Everything was in its proper place. As for my appearance, my hair and clothing were disheveled. I looked like I had been through a war.

During the session, I was not asked any questions about my mental occurrences. Like what kinds of thoughts reverberated through your mind, or at this moment are you experiencing uncontrollable thoughts, or have you ever wanted to commit suicide? No questions at all. The doctor asked Tim what kind of changes caused my predicament. Tim stated he noticed a difference in my attitude when I started to read the Holy Bible more. He talked about it in an adverse manner. During interval moments, the therapist stared at me as he listened and provided Tim with uh huhs. My counseling session turned out to be a dialogue between Tim and my doctor. When I think back, there was no need for me to be there because they spoke as if I was not in the room.

I was shocked and speechless at Tim's response. I wanted to scream at the top of my lungs: "Don't believe him! That's not true! Don't blame additional bible study times as the cause of my mental attacks." If anything, the words of God provided me with hope to strive in every aspect of my life and the stamina to raise my children.

I wanted Tim to confess the trauma that he kept bringing into my life. Tell the Doctor how you steal from your wife and children. Tell the Doctor how you give our money to the drug dealers. Tell the Doctor how many houses we had lost due to your drug habits. Tell the Doctor how your actions caused bankruptcies and car repossessions. Tell the Doctor how you continue to rob us of our our family vacations. Tell the Doctor how we do not have enough money for proper dental care. Tell the Doctor how we are always low on funds. Tell the Doctor that I barely have the appropriate monthly female products. Tell the Doctor how we live from paycheck to paycheck. Tell the Doctor how every single payday we are broke.

Tell the Doctor how we lack quality food, clothing, and other necessities of life. Tell the Doctor how your wife cries as she searches for aids to keep our household utilities from being disconnected. Tell the Doctor how I sometimes have to beg for lunch money. Tell the Doctor about my looks of horror and disappointment whenever the water, electricity, or telephone services are turned off. Tell the Doctor how I have suppressed my emotions within me for many years. Tell the Doctor how some of my family members laugh at me and the children in our hand-me down clothes.

Tell the Doctor how I have to cry myself to sleep many nights. Tell the Doctor all I want is for my children to live in a stable environment. Tell the Doctor how I always have to carry the heavy load of our family's responsibilities. Tell the Doctor that our life is like a brown paper bag with a hole at the bottom of it; everything we put into it falls through it. Tell the Doctor how you keep promising me that things are going to get better. Tell the Doctor about your disappearing acts. Tell the Doctor how I silently keep the pain of your wrong doings within me. Tell the Doctor that I can't handle any more of your deceitful lies.

After their conversation had ended, my doctor told Tim that I had suffered from a nervous breakdown. I was summoned to follow him into the back of his office. He asked me to select between two anti-depressant medications. He verbally spoke their names and asked me to quickly select one of them. I was clueless. I thought, "aren't you the doctor? Why are you showing me two different kinds of anti-depressant medications without any descriptions about them? Why should I select something that I am oblivious to? You stated that I had experienced a nervous breakdown. Why can't you recommend one of them? Then, you can properly explain the reason why you selected it."

His actions confirmed my suspicion. I knew something was inappropriate about him. From the initial start of my session, I didn't get a good vibe from him. Also, I didn't feel it was a safe environment. To get away from him, I pointed towards one of the medications. I was given the prescription. We walked back into the front of his office. He said a couple of other words to Tim. The therapist acted very unprofessionally. However, he doesn't represent other therapists who truly care about their patients.

After my appointment, Tim and I walked toward the elevator. He didn't ask what the doctor and I talked about, or about the prescription that was in my hand. My husband had other things on his mind. He wanted to catch a cab and to get back to work. At that moment, I needed to talk to him. I was disturbed and disappointed about the entire doctor's visit. When we entered the lobby of the building, he said good-bye and dashed out of the building. I walked over to the window and watched him as he flagged down a taxi. I felt all alone. I looked at the man that I chose to marry, and I sadly shook my head. I knew that I had to be strong for my children and myself. Deep within I knew our marriage was coming to an end.

I walked over to the pharmacy located in the same building. While I stood in line waiting to give my prescription to the pharmacist clerk, my sons ran toward me saying "Mommie, Mommie." The sound of their voices distracted my melancholy mood. I bent down to greet them with my arms wide open. I gave them a loving hug. Yes, I gained strength from their voices. These babies were given to me by God. They needed their mother to be strong and healthy. Deep within, I knew without a doubt that I was going to be alright. We were going to make it. My dad looked at how I interacted with my sons and smiled. He was our biggest fan.

In the pharmacy, there was a man watching us. He marched over to me as if he was on a mission. He stopped and looked me straight in my eyes. He said, "you are a beautiful African queen – you have to take care of these princes. Do you hear me? I said to take care of these princes." He abruptly turned and walked out of the pharmacy doors. Clearly the man knew that I had suffered through something. It was obvious by my appearance. He knew my children needed their mother. It was his way to encourage me to stay strong. God has a mighty sweet way of bringing things all together.

After three days of taking the anti-depressant medication. I decided to stop using them. I said, "God I know that you are a healer. I ask you to continue to heal me. By faith, I trust in you." I discarded the pills and never looked back. It has been over 30 years of not taking any anti-depressant medication. Only God can completely heal in this capacity. I continue to thank the Almighty for a clean slate and a healthy mind.

Did my complete healing restoration happen overnight? No, it did not. Each day, I gained strength spiritually, mentally, and physically. Some days it felt like I was not going to make it. My faith in God allowed me to believe and hope for a brighter future. That's when I received the spiritual fortitude to continue to believe that my healing had already taken place. I was walking through the natural process of it. His gentle hand guided me through every step of the way, and He gave me victory over a nervous breakdown.

My Daddy the One who I loved!

My father passed away Friday, June 12, 2009. This was one of the saddest days of my life. Since his death, the world has not been the same. I loved him so much. My family and I were blessed to have him in our lives. My brothers will agree that our father was a generous and kind-hearted man. His love was infectious. The day before he passed away, I had a chance to say how much I loved him. I told my daddy how I thanked God for selecting him to be my father.

In the same month as my father's death, I was granted a divorce decree from Ned. It did not weigh me down. I was at a place of wholeness. I was determined to live my life to the fullest.

The valuable words of my beloved Father, Elder Nehemiah Dean Smith Jr, "the fight is fixed. Jesus has already worked it out. Twinkles, release your tumultuous past and move forward daughter." This is exactly what I am doing.

Dear Daddy,

I never doubted your love. I forgave you for not being strong enough to protect me from my mother's eccentric behavior. I know that you were badly affected too. Your life was filled with hurt and disappointments, but you did not run from adversities. I want to apologize to you Daddy, for you didn't get a chance to accomplish some of your natural goals. Yet, you were not angry against anyone, not even yourself.

Daddy, thank you for being so good to your family. Your positivity and patience were the epitome of your love for us. Your treasured words have left a tremendous impact in our lives. Even as of today, your words continue to inspire and encourage us. We will never forget your smile.

Truly, God gave us one of his special jewels when he gave you to us. You Daddy – You were that precious gift. Your relationship with the Heavenly Father blessed us all. We saw how you walked, talked, and lived the life of a believer in Christ Jesus. You were filled with true joy. Thank you for your kindness. Thank you for

being an illustration of an earthly rock. Thank you for leaving an enriched spiritual legacy to your family.
With the deepest of love
Your daughter, Twinkles

Father, some of the readers are grieving the death of a loved one or friend, strengthen them. Earth has no sorrow which Heaven can't heal. I ask you to bend down on one knee and wrap your arms of love around them. Cover them with your comfort and peace. Let your anointed words of encouragement penetrate to the deepest parts of their hearts.

O Mighty LORD, you created the mind and its functions. There are some readers who suffer from emotional disorders. Release your supernatural healing power to every inch of their minds and bodies. God, thank you for working inconceivable miracles. And it is so, in Christ Jesus' name.

CHAPTER TWELVE
THANK YOU MOMMIE

So if the Son sets you free, you will be free indeed
(John 8:36)

Daddy and mama were married for almost fifty years. Six years after his death, my mama passed away Sunday, June 21, 2015. One of my favorite female cousins, Jennifer, called and informed me about her death. I remember being totally numb and sad. To be honest, I didn't cry at all. There was not one tear that fell from my eyes. Instead, my mind flashed to former memories of our complicated relationship. All of the pleading and begging her to love me. Countless overwhelming telephone conversations which led to relentless condemnation and dreadful thoughts. After we ended our strenuous dialog, I was drained and depressed. My very own mama petrified me.

There were times when I cried before scheduled visits with mama. I never knew what kind of mood she would be in. While in her presence, I searched for ways to escape. My mother didn't like me, and I detested her ways. I was once asked a question. Daffney, why do you subject yourself to toxicity? My answer was "because she is my mother."

I would have loved to see my mother filled with glee, bubbly about the prospect of her life. God knows I wanted this special wish for my mama. There were special moments when I prayed, encouraged and shared positive words with her. She agreed and accepted my prayers. Surprisingly, when I got ordained as a minister, my mother acknowledged my spiritual calling from God. This was the only decision of mine that she didn't fight against. She confessed and accepted Christ Jesus as her Savior. Unfortunately, there are some people who are saved but live defeated lives on earth. They refuse to accept Him as both Savior and Lord. They do not acknowledge Him as their Lord. As a consequence, they are guided by their own emotions and feelings. They face difficult trials and life-changing decisions through their own strength. This is a tragedy.

In my mother's honor, I wanted to give her a good home going celebration service. I made sure her funeral service was organized and filled with harmonizing songs. Mama loved gospel quartets and old-time gospel songs. She and daddy sat at our kitchen table listening to music. I remember one of their favorite's singers, was Lee William and the Spiritual QC's. I liked his music too.

My brothers, appointed relatives and friends took care of other aspects of her funeral arrangements. My brother, Gerald, preceded my mother in death. The morning of her funeral brought turmoil filled with torrential rain. When I looked out of the hotel's automatic doors, the streaming flow of the rain drops distracted me. It jolted more painful memories. Nevertheless, I was able to relinquish the negative thoughts from my mind (at least for the moment). I had to maintain a positive disposition at her funeral. My mother's funeral service was good. After the funeral procession left the cemetery, I sat by her gravesite for a little while longer. My children and two friends stayed with me. They wanted to know if I was okay. I was fine, for my mama could not hurt me anymore.

After her death, I experienced a season of quietness. There was no talk of criticism of others. There was no guilt and sadness. There was no degradation. There were no outbursts. There were no indirect remarks about not being a caring daughter. However, there was still a part of me silently crying out for my Mommie.

She was a distant woman who happened to be my mother. I longed for her to say, "Twinkles, mama loves you." I longed for mama to allow me to cry on her shoulders. I longed for those mother and daughter heart to heart conversations. I longed for her not to only be my mother but my friend too. I never asked to be her "loveless daughter." She gave this hideous title to me, and I carried it until she passed away.

In certain times of crisis, my mama was there for me. She expressed her love through the demonstration of helpful acts. I loved having her on my side. Even though, her assistance was based on stipulations and temporary circumstances. It never failed. As soon as my immediate emergencies were resolved, her attacks against me resurfaced slowly. Then, she reverted to the same controlling and disrespectful person. Her devious attacks against me caused a lot of confusion and stress. All she needed was a person's ear to share my personal flaws with. For some unfathomable reason, this made mama happy.

It took a long time for me to discover the emptiness that my mother carried from her childhood. It was the reason why she behaved in such an inappropriate manner. Mommie was unloved, rejected, and not properly cared for by her father. The absence of his affections truly wounded her. As a result, she harbored anger and bitterness toward him. Deep down within, she longed for his love and acceptance. Like me, she too was a "loveless daughter."

Mama gave to her family what was given to her....P-A-I-N – Emotional Pain. Because my mother was not celebrated, she did not know how to affectionately love her husband and children. The whole time I thought it was my fault, but her deep-rooted anger grew from unresolved issues from her childhood struggles. By association, I was pulled by force into my mother and grandfather's whirlwind of dysfunction. It was a vicious cycle.

Three years and one day after my mama passed away. I was scheduled to fly to California for a Trauma Healing Facilitator Training. The evening before my flight, I thought about my mother. I cried and wailed for hours. Then, something lovely occurred. The heaviness from my heart was removed, and I was cleansed and filled with pure affection for my mama. Each tear produced a greater love for her. I didn't want to stop crying, for it was liberating.

For the first time, I grieved the death of my mother. Each year prior, I did not acknowledge any of her death anniversaries. I erased them from my mind. This was the appointed time for me to properly mourn her death. I continued to cry until I remembered that I had a scheduled nail appointment. I figure that I could defer my mourning to later that night. I needed to take care of business. I got myself together as much as possible. Let me tell you my plan didn't work, because I cried at the nail salon. I was barely able to tell my nail technician, Seena, why I was crying. I mustered enough strength to inform her about my mother's death anniversary. I told her that I would be fine. Just let me cry. She motioned for me to sit down. As she worked on my nails, I cried and used a lot of anti-bacterial hand gel, and a lot of Kleenex tissues. There were other women at the nail salon shop too. Seena made sure no one bothered me. After she finished with my nails, she gave me a loving hug.

When I returned to my car, one of my friends returned my telephone call. I was still crying when I answered the telephone. I let her know that I was not sad but thankful. I was giving praise unto God! I finally have a genuine love for my mother. Not only had I forgiven her – I loved her dearly. All the negativity was removed, and I was free. Doreé immediately prayed for me, and we praised God for His awesome work of emotional healing.

The bottom line was, she was my mama. The only mother that I had. The first lady of my life. Through the power of the Holy Spirit, I was taught how to love her even in death. I stopped focusing and talking about her destructive ways. I saw her as a broken individual. It became easier to concentrate on her good qualities.

I realized that she did her best. It was all she had to give. Mama could not give me 100%, because she only had 40% to give.

Mama's Last words before Death

My mama's last words spoken to me were, "you are so beautiful; you are so beautiful." I froze. I was not expecting to hear these lovely words from her. She was laying in her bed with a radiant smile planted on her face. Both of us smiled at each other. I walked closer to her and sat on the edge of the bed. She reached up to hold on to one of my shirt sleeves. We sat quietly looking into each other eyes. This was a very special and rare moment. My mother stared at me with eyes of love. Even now, I get very emotional when I think about our last encounter. In retrospect, I had no idea that this was her silent way of saying goodbye; I am proud of you and I love you. I see the beauty that is inside of you.

One day while cleaning, I found an old birthday card that mama had given to me. The card was colorful and beautifully decorated. The front of it had seven large printed words written on it. Darling, Ambitious, Gorgeous, Hardworking, Talented, Entertaining, and Remarkable. Inside of the card, it read, "you wonder why we can't stop bragging about you." Mama wrote, "Happy Birthday from your Mother - Love you – God is Love." It is the only thing that I have left with her handwriting on it. I was touched. I cherish this card. Mama loved me in her own special way. One of my aunts told me before my mother passed away, mama wanted her sisters to call each of her children to make sure we were alright. Her words comforted me.

Mama my Hero

When I was in the first grade, mama felt that I was too young to walk home alone. Therefore, she walked with me to school. I noticed that a lot of the other neighborhood children walked together as a group without their parents. I wanted to be a big girl. This prompted me to beg mama to grant me permission to walk home by myself. She agreed and described some of our front yard landmarks. She said, "Twinkles, we have a large tree near our front gate and two smaller trees near the front windows." I listened and placed a mental note of the landmarks into my mind. I told her that I understood her instructions.

The next day, I was happy. I thought today is the day that I become a big girl. I was going to walk home with the other neighborhood children without the presence of my mama. The things that bring happiness to a first grader. When the school day ended, I walked and talked with the other school children. Our group started to dwindle as each child got closer to his or her house. However, I kept talking until there was no one left to converse with.

After a while, I noticed that I was lost. I continued to search for my house. I rehearsed the landmarks within in my mind, I could not remember them. Then, I cried and panicked, because I could not find my house. I did not see anyone who could help me, so I continued to cry for my mother's help. My whole little world had crumbled down. I had no idea how to resolve my issue. Eventually, a stranger came and asked what was wrong. Talking between sobs, I told the person that I could not find where I lived, and I wanted my Mommie.

The person calmed me down and promised to help me find my house. We searched for my house together; the stranger's kind voice asked me "Is this where you live?" I sobbed and answered "No." As we continued to walk, I eventually remembered my house's landmarks. The closer I got to it, I saw my mama. She stood in our front yard with a concerned look on her face. I was relieved to see her. I called her name, and I ran to her. She opened her arms wide toward me, and I ran into them. I felt safe in her loving arms. I calmed down, and we stood out front of our yard for a little while, thrilled to see each other and to be in each other's company again. It was as if we hadn't seen one another for a very long time.

Mama wanted to know how I found my way home? Caught up into the excitement, I forgot someone was with me. As I turned and looked for the stranger who held my hand and guided me home, that person was nowhere in sight. I told mama about the stranger who volunteered to help me. She had a puzzled look on her face. As a mother, I understand now why she was baffled to have a young child who got lost and was in the hands of a stranger. That's scary. I knew she was relieved that nothing bad happened to me.

To this day, I have no idea who held my hand and guided me home. Maybe it was my guardian angel. One thing is for sure, God knows the identity of the individual. I am happy that a kind stranger helped me. After this incident, mama resumed walking me to school. I welcomed it. After a couple of years, I was given permission to walk home without a chaperone. I knew exactly where I lived and never got lost again. This story is special because it is one of my fondest memories of feeling safe in my mother's arms.

Dear Mama,

I love you. I know that you experienced many unfavorable circumstances in your life. Your dreams were suppressed into the deepest places of your existence. Unfortunately, they laid in dormant and withered away. Mama, you settled for less. I know you were wounded. I get it. However, I must be bold in what I am about to say. You took on a victim mentality. You gave up. You fought the ones who truly loved you. I know – deception gives all of us erroneous thoughts. Certainly, I was not your enemy.

Thank you Mommie

Thank you for being my mother. Thank you for birthing me into the world. Thank you for greeting me with a smile and a soft touch. Thank you for being there when my children and I needed you. I remember times when I didn't have money to purchase Christmas toys for them. You spent some of your Christmas bonus funds to help purchase their gifts. You didn't want your grandchildren to be deprived from having a good day. On Christmas Eve day, we went shopping to find toys. It was a busy day. The lines in the stores were long, but for some reason it didn't faze you. You did not complain. During those times, we worked in unity. We were a good team. Christmas Day morning, the children opened their gifts with gratitude. Thank you for sending my daddy to bring bags of groceries to us.

Mama, thank you for having such great taste in clothing and shoes. You were a very classy dresser. I honestly got that from you. At the age of twelve, I borrowed your high heel shoes without permission. I used them to walk to the end of our neighborhood mailbox. I was determined to walk straight in those high heel shoes without falling on my behind. Successfully, I accomplished both of those goals. I overheard you bragging to one of our neighbors how I impressed you. Because, I was able to walk steady in high heels shoes. Your compliment placed a smile on my face. Little did you know that I had plenty of practice. Many of our neighbors already knew about my shoe excursions.

Thank you for teaching me some etiquette. You stated that young ladies should never be loud, and I should always carry myself like a lady. I listened to your helpful tips. I am a sophisticated woman and a southern belle in mannerism. Mama, I pause as I get ready to say these words to you. Although you cannot hear them, I publicly share them before countless people. While you were living, I didn't get a chance to ask you for forgiveness. Please forgive me for anything that I have done against you. The Father let me know, as I forgave you, I was set free.

Dorothy Olinda Smith, you are at rest in the arms of Christ Jesus. Finally, mama rest in His peace!

I love you Mommie,
Your daughter, Twinkles

A few years before mama passed away, I was prompted by the Spirit of God to tell her that she was a good mother. In addition, I was to say how she did her best. Mama received my compliments with tears welled up in her eyes. These words were poignant, and they touched her profoundly. I am glad that I was obedient.

My younger son, Teron, served in the United States Navy. I was very proud of him. He married his high school sweetheart Brenda. At the time, I didn't want them to get married because they were young. Nevertheless, they decided to get married. I made up my mind to be the best mother-in-law to Brenda. I left it up to her to receive or reject my love. She accepted it.

Brenda has brought a lot of love and sunshine into our family. Toney and Travis adore their sister-in-love. That girl loves them too. When they talk by telephone or in person, there is a lot of laughter, giggles, and excitement.

God gives beauty for ashes. Since I didn't have a close knitted relationship with my mother, He compensated me with an amazing relationship with my daughter-in-love Brenda. Love always wins. Brenda and I like to give each other gifts. One day, she made a pink and white poster for me. She is very creative. It reads, "Where you go, I will go. Where you stay, I will stay, your God will be my God. I love you Minnie (term of endearment)." She ended her treasure-filled words by drawing a heart symbol. The poster serves as a reminder of her pledge to love me. Brenda is my bonus child. I thank her mother, Victoria, for generously sharing her gift from heaven with me.

As I approach the end of my book, I can still hear the words of my oldest son Toney's profound advice, "Mom when you write your book keep it real, so that other people can get free." Toney, I kept it real.

Father, I praise your Holy name. I have shared what you wanted me to disclose. Each reader was on your mind as you directed me to write this book. You have made an irrevocable promise to deliver every born-again believer from the captivity of brokenness to the victory of wholeness. I serve as a witness that God does exactly what He says. Shalom!

FROM BROKENNESS TO WHOLENESS

WORDS FROM PROPHETESS DAFFNEY M. HAWKINS

PRESIDENT OF ONLY THE KING CAN DO IT MINISTRY, INC.

Rejection catapulted me into the arms of a loving God. In Him, I am truly safe. The Lord broke my invisible chains and removed my handcuffs. He freed me from my bondages. By His Holy Spirit, I am determined not to go backward but to keep moving forward.

I went from living in Brokenness to thriving in Wholeness. I am literally in awe of His wondrous working powers. God's love and affection sweeps over my soul. I am immersed in His unconditional love.

The Holy Spirit revealed some interesting facts about my childhood traumatic car accident. The strange voice that I heard served as a warning that my life was in jeopardy. The peace that saturated me in my bedroom was the presence of God. It was His reassurance to me that everything was going to be fine. It was a near-death experience. "The moment your head hit the concrete, you stepped into the presence of the Lord. I spoke breath back into your lifeless body. I rescued you from death; it was not your time." The hospital's window scene "darkness turning into light" within seconds was one of His phenomena for me to witness. He is the creator of the universe and beyond. God can use any of it to express His greatness. *(Amos 5:8)* Years later, my first speaking engagement invitation was from a Pastor who church was located on the same street where my car accident happened.

Many of you are still in some form of brokenness. You have tried everything to get free, yet the depression and stress continue to linger on. I recommend Christ Jesus. Not only will He be your Savior and Lord - God will be your friend too! He can help you - like He helped me. You don't have to live another day in fear. The Father has promised not to leave or forsake you. No one in this world can say he or she won't leave you. There are some promises that we can't keep, but God can. He never wanted you to suffer. Due to a broken world system, there are lots of unfortunate situations. It seems like things are getting worse.

However, we are not left without hope. God is the hope of glory. In Him, our expectations are fulfilled. There is nothing like being in His will. You can talk to the Creator of the Universe at any given time. His ears are never heavy nor closed. Day or night, He is always there. The Ancient of Days, He never sleeps nor slumbers. The Father is willing and ready to bless you with His grace and mercy. Don't let the distractions keep you from knowing Him. The Father is waiting for you. **NEVER GIVE UP!**

SCRIPTURE REFERENCE

But when the kindness and the love of God our Savior toward man appeared, not by works of righteousness which we have done, but according to His mercy, He saved us, through the washing of regeneration and renewing of the Holy Spirit *(Titus 3:4-5)*

Because of his great love for us, God, who is rich in mercy, made us alive with Christ even when we were dead in transgressions-it is by grace you have been saved. *(Ephesians 2:4-5)*

For though we live in the world, we do not wage war as the world does. The weapons we fight with are not the weapons of the world. On the contrary, they have divine power to demolish strongholds. We demolish arguments and every pretension that sets itself up against the knowledge of God, and we take captive every thought to make it obedient to Christ. And we will be ready to punish every act of disobedience, once your obedience is complete.
(2 Corinthians 10:3-6)

God made him who had no sin to be sin for us, so that in him we might become the righteousness of God. *(2 Corinthians 5:21)*

For all the promises of God in him are yea, and in him Amen, unto the glory of God by us. *(2 Corinthians 1:20)*

Having been buried with him in baptism, in which you were also raised with him through your faith in the working of God, who raised him from the dead. *(Colossians 2:12)*

And then he told them, "Go into all the world and preach the Good News to everyone. Whoever believes and is baptized will be saved, but whoever does not believe will be condemned. *(Mark 16:15-16)*

If you declare with your mouth, "Jesus is LORD," and believe in your heart that God raised him from the dead, you will be saved. *(Romans 10:9)*

And in Him, having heard and believed the word of truth—the gospel of your salvation—you were sealed with the promised Holy Spirit. *(Ephesians 1:13)*

So he said to me, "This is the word of the LORD to Zerubbabel: 'Not by might nor by power, but by my Spirit,' says the LORD Almighty. *(Zechariah 4:6)*

God is not man, that he should lie, or a son of man, that he should change his mind. Has he said, and will he not do it? Or has he spoken, and will he not fulfill it? *(Numbers 23:19)*

But you, O Lord, are a merciful and gracious God, slow to anger and abounding in steadfast love and faithfulness. *(Psalm 86:15)*

Trust in the Lord with all your heart and lean not on your own understanding; in all your ways submit to him, and he will make your paths straight. *(Proverbs 3:5-6)*

Now this is the confidence that we have in Him, that if we ask anything according to His will, He hears us. And if we know that He hears us, whatever we ask, we know that we have the petitions that we have asked of Him. *(1 John 5:14-15)*

For we live by faith, not by sight. *(2 Corinthians 5:7)*

Whoever believes in me, as Scripture has said, rivers of living water will flow from within them. *(John 7:38)*

Jesus looked at them and said, "With man this is impossible, but not with God; all things are possible with God." *(Mark 10:27)*

Have faith in God, Jesus answered. Truly I tell you, if anyone says to this mountain, "Go, throw yourself into the sea,' and does not doubt in their heart but believes that what they say will happen, it will be done for them. Therefore, I tell you, whatever you ask for in prayer, believe that you have received it, and it will be yours. And when you stand praying, if you hold anything against anyone, forgive them, so that your Father in heaven may forgive you your sins." *(Mark 11:22-25)*

For if you forgive other people when they sin against you, your Heavenly Father will also forgive you. But if you do not forgive others their sins, your Father will not forgive your sins. *(Matthew 6:14-15)*

He reveals deep and hidden things; he knows what lies in darkness, and light dwells with him. *(Daniel 2:22)*

He will sit as a refiner and purifier of silver, and he will purify the sons of Levi and refine them like gold and silver, and they will bring offerings in righteousness to the LORD. *(Malachi 3:3)*

For the LORD God is a sun and shield; the LORD bestows favor and honor; no good thing does he withhold from those whose walk is blameless. *(Psalm 84:11)*

Don't be afraid, for I am with you. Don't be discouraged, for I am your God. I will strengthen you and help you. I will hold you up with my victorious right hand. *(Isaiah 41:10)*

Lord, you are my God; I will exalt you and praise your name, for in perfect faithfulness you have done wonderful things, things planned long ago. *(Isaiah 25:1)*

Taste and see that the Lord is good; blessed is the one who takes refuge in him. *(Psalm 34:8)*

"For my thoughts are not your thoughts, neither are your ways my ways," declares the Lord. *(Isaiah 55:8)*

The temptations in your life are no different from what others experience. And God is faithful. He will not allow the temptation to be more than you can stand. When you are tempted, he will show you a way out so that you can endure. *(1 Corinthians 10:13)*

The name of the LORD is a strong tower; the righteous man runs into it and is safe. *(Proverbs 18:10)*

Be strong and courageous. Do not be afraid or terrified because of them, for the LORD your God goes with you; he will never leave you nor forsake you. *(Deuteronomy 31:6)*

I love those who love me, and those who seek me find me. *(Proverbs 8:17)*

For I am not ashamed of the gospel, because it is the power of God that brings salvation to everyone who believes: first to the Jew, then to the Gentile. *(Romans 1:16)*

The thief comes only to steal and kill and destroy; I have come that they may have life and have it to the full. *(John 10:10)*

You belong to your father, the devil, and you want to carry out your father's desires. He was a murderer from the beginning, not holding to the truth, for there is no truth in him. When he lies, he speaks his native language, for he is a liar and the father of lies. *(John 8:44)*

You will also declare a thing, and it will be established for you; So light will shine on your ways. *(Job 22:28)*

No weapon forged against you will prevail, and you will refute every tongue that accuses you. This is the heritage of the servants of the LORD, and this is their vindication from me," declares the LORD. *(Isaiah 54:17)*

When the enemy comes in like a flood, The Spirit of the LORD will lift up a standard against him. *(Isaiah 59:19)*

He who finds a wife finds what is good and receives favor from the LORD. *(Proverbs 18:22)*

For He spoke, and it came to be; He commanded, and it stood firm. (Psalm 33:9)

Now in the sixth month the angel Gabriel was sent by God to a city of Galilee named Nazareth, to a virgin betrothed to a man whose name was Joseph, of the house of David. The virgin's name was Mary. And having come in, the angel said to her, "Rejoice, highly favored one, the Lord is with you; blessed are you among women!" But when she saw him, she was troubled at his saying, and considered what manner of greeting this was. Then the angel said to her, "Do not be afraid, Mary, for you have found favor with God. And behold, you will conceive in your womb and bring forth a Son, and shall call His name JESUS. He will be great, and will be called the Son of the Highest; and the Lord God will give Him the throne of His father David. And He will reign over the house of Jacob forever, and of His kingdom there will be no end." Then Mary said to the angel, "How can this be, since I do not know a man?" And the angel answered and said to her, "The Holy Spirit will come upon you, and the power of the Highest will overshadow you; therefore, also, that Holy One who is to be born will be called the Son of God. *(Luke 1:26-35)*

Keep this Book of the Law always on your lips; meditate on it day and night, so that you may be careful to do everything written in it. Then you will be prosperous and successful. *(Joshua 1:8)*

God is Spirit, and those who worship Him must worship in spirit and truth. *(John 4:24)*

Therefore it is of faith that it might be according to grace, so that the promise might be sure to all the seed, not only to those who are of the law, but also to those who are of the faith of Abraham, who is the father of us all (as it is written, "I have made you a father of many nations") in the presence of Him whom he believed—God, who gives life to the dead and calls those things which do not exist as though they did; who, contrary to hope, in hope believed, so that he became the father of many nations, according to what was spoken, "So shall your descendants be." *(Romans 4:16-18)*

Bear with each other and forgive one another if any of you has a grievance against someone. Forgive as the Lord forgave you. *(Colossians 3:13)*

My son, if you receive my words, and treasure my commands within you, so that you incline your ear to wisdom, a*nd* apply your heart to understanding; yes, if you cry out for discernment, *And* lift up your voice for understanding, If you seek her as silver, and search for her as *for* hidden treasures; then you will understand the fear of the LORD, and find the knowledge of God. For the LORD gives wisdom; from His mouth *come* knowledge and understanding; He stores up sound wisdom for the upright; h*e is* a shield to those who walk uprightly; He guards the paths of justice, and preserves the way of His saints. Then you will understand righteousness and justice, equity *and* every good path. *(Proverbs 2:1-9)*

For unto us a Child is born, unto us a Son is given; and the government will be upon His shoulder. and His name will be called Wonderful, Counselor, Mighty God, Everlasting Father, Prince of Peace. *(Isaiah 9:6)*

He has shown you, O man, what *is* good; and what does the LORD require of you But to do justly, to love mercy, and to walk humbly with your God? *(Micah 6:8)*

Greater love has no one than this: to lay down one's life for one's friends. *(John 15:13)*

But you are a chosen people, a royal priesthood, a holy nation, God's special possession, that you may declare the praises of him who called you out of darkness into his wonderful light. *(1 Peter 2:9)*

When the Spirit of truth comes, he will guide you into all the truth, for he will not speak on his own authority, but whatever he hears he will speak, and he will declare to you the things that are to come. *(John 16:13)*

May the God of hope fill you with all joy and peace as you trust in him, so that you may overflow with hope by the power of the Holy Spirit. *(Romans 15:13)*

The grace of the Lord Jesus Christ, and the love of God, and the fellowship of the Holy Spirit, be with you all. *(2 Corinthians 13:14)*

We love Him because He first loved us. *(1 John 4:19)*

The blessing of the LORD makes one rich, And He adds no sorrow with it. *(Proverbs 10:22)*

THE PURPOSE OF BROKENNESS TO WHOLENESS

For I know the thoughts that I think toward you, says the Lord, thoughts of peace and not of evil, to give you a future and a hope. Then you will call upon Me and go and pray to Me, and I will listen to you. And you will seek Me and find Me, when you search for Me with all your heart. (Jeremiah 29:11-13) This book is to be utilized as a tool for the witnessing of Christ Jesus. Its main purpose is to serve others with healing, deliverance and the restoration power of God.

Daffney's testimony is shared in a prolific and courageous manner. She expresses the process of her tumultuous journey from brokenness to wholeness. By grace, her impossibilities were replaced by possibilities in Christ Jesus. Also, it provides the hopefulness of God to timely rescue anyone from the snares of bondage. The soundness of its wisdom encourages, inspires and motivates anyone to discover his or her voice. It guarantees to help others to avoid spiritual and natural pitfalls.

She has been given a mantle to feed the people of God and others with the good news of Christ Jesus. Her ministry continues to reach into the deepest part of the Earth. She is a motivator and an inspirational speaker. Her deepest desire is to see everyone set free and delivered from the kingdom of darkness to the kingdom of light.

Her ministry is based in Jeffersonville, PA. This woman of God is on the cutting edge. She is doing phenomenal things in the Kingdom of God! Daffney knows without God she is nothing.

For more information about her ministry, please visit www.okcdim.org.